Corporate Acquisitions and Mergers in Singapore

Corporate Acquisitions and Mergers in Singapore

Fourth Edition

Andrew M. Lim
Lim Mei
Richard Young
Christopher Ong
Daren Shiau
Sunit Chhabra
Lim Pek Bur
Yeo Boon Kiat

Allen & Gledhill LLP

This book was originally published as a chapter in Corporate Acquisitions and Mergers.

General Editor: Peter Begg

Wolters Kluwer

Published by:
Kluwer Law International B.V.
PO Box 316
2400 AH Alphen aan den Rijn
The Netherlands
E-mail: lrs-sales@wolterskluwer.com
Website: www.wolterskluwer.com/en/solutions/kluwerlawinternational

Sold and distributed by:
Wolters Kluwer Legal & Regulatory U.S.
7201 McKinney Circle
Frederick, MD 21704
United States of America
E-mail: customer.service@wolterskluwer.com

ISBN 978-94-035-0306-6

e-Book: ISBN 978-94-035-0596-1
web-PDF: ISBN 978-94-035-0606-7

Contents

Allen & Gledhill LLP

Allen & Gledhill is an award-winning full-service Southeast Asian law firm which provides legal services to premier clients, including local and multinational corporations and financial institutions. The Firm was established in 1902 and is consistently ranked in band one of the market leaders in Singapore and Southeast Asia, having been involved in a number of challenging, complex and significant deals, many of which are first of its kind. The Firm's reputation for high-quality service is regularly affirmed by the strong rankings in leading publications, and by the various awards and accolades, it has received from independent commentators and clients. The Firm is consistently ranked one in the highest number of practice areas and is one of the firms with the highest number of lawyers recognized as leading individuals. Over the years, the Firm has also been named 'Regional Law Firm of the Year' and 'SE Asia Law Firm of the Year' by many prominent legal publishers. With a growing network of associate firms and offices, Allen & Gledhill is well-placed to advise clients on their business interests in Singapore and beyond, in particular, on matters involving Southeast Asia and the Asian region. With its offices in Singapore, Myanmar and Vietnam, as well as its associate firm in Malaysia, Rahmat Lim & Partners, and its network firm in Indonesia, Soemadipradja & Taher, the Allen & Gledhill network has over 650 lawyers in the region, making it one of the largest law firms in Southeast Asia.

As one of the largest full-service firms in Singapore, we are able to offer breadth and depth in terms of specialist legal experts and resources to assist our Corporate M&A practice to navigate issues and provide solutions on various aspects of the law that inevitably arise in an M&A transaction. These specialist practices are themselves individually recognized as leading practices and include Competition, Corporate Real Estate, Corporate Services, Financial Services, Intellectual Property and Tax.

All these specialist areas are helmed by Partners who are recognized leaders in their respective fields. Their strengths and expertise are thereby leveraged upon by our Corporate M&A practice with confidence. In this vein, our Corporate M&A practice has extensive expertise and a proven record of coordinating and structuring legal services and advice across a number of specialist areas, presenting them to our clients in a seamless and integrated form.

Our Corporate M&A team is the leading practice in Singapore and the region and stands apart in terms of size and expertise. Our Corporate M&A practice offers a breadth of personnel, skills and resources, as well as depth of bench through the expertise and experience of our Corporate M&A Partners.

We have a dedicated Corporate M&A team of twenty-five Partners, making us one of the largest M&A teams in Singapore and Southeast Asia. Our team has advised and acted as lead counsel on many of the most challenging, complex and high profile M&A transactions in Singapore and the region, of which involve cross-border elements.

Our Corporate M&A Partners include some of the top M&A practitioners who, over the years, have actively led the market in pioneering deal structures and handling innovative matters, many of which have set industry standards and market best practices.

Authors

Andrew M. Lim is a senior partner of Allen & Gledhill LLP and a member of the firm's Executive Committee. He was admitted to the Singapore Bar in 1986.

Andrew has been consistently recognized for his expertise and as a leading lawyer in his field. He has, over the course of almost thirty years in practice, advised clients on numerous strategic and market-leading corporate, restructuring and commercial transactions, and on corporate governance, regulatory and compliance matters.

E-mail: andrew.lim@allenandgledhill.com

Phone: 6890 7706

Lim Mei is the Co-Head of the Corporate Mergers & Acquisitions Department at Allen & Gledhill.

Her areas of practice include mergers and acquisitions, equity capital markets and derivatives. She has extensive experience in mergers and acquisitions and has advised on numerous landmark domestic and cross-border mergers and acquisitions. She is also actively involved in the listing of nearly all of the structured warrant programmes on the Singapore Exchange. Her clients include large-cap companies, multinational corporations, sovereign wealth funds, financial institutions and private equity firms.

Lim Mei has been a Partner with the Firm since 1996.

E-mail: lim.mei@allenandgledhill.com

Phone: 6890 7732

Richard Young has extensive experience in domestic and cross-border mergers and acquisitions (with a particular focus on share and business acquisitions), local and regional joint ventures, schemes of arrangements, amalgamations, capital reductions, corporate reorganizations as well as general corporate and commercial law.

He has been cited for his expertise in mergers and acquisitions and recognized as a leading individual for Corporate/M&A in legal publications such as *Chambers Global* and *Chambers Asia-Pacific*. He is also noted for his work in M&A by *IFLR1000*.

He joined Allen & Gledhill on a scholarship in 1995 and became a Partner in 2000.

E-mail: richard.young@allenandgledhill.com

Phone: 6890 7635

Christopher Ong's areas of expertise span private and public take-overs, banking transfers and private equity transactions.

He has extensive experience acting for offerors and target companies in public takeovers, schemes of arrangements and delistings. His practice involves advising listed issuers on their regulatory and compliance work.

His experience encompasses banking transfers, having advised financial institutions on both the acquisition and disposal of banking business.

E-mail: christopher.ong@allenandgledhill.com

Phone: 6890 7728

Daren Shiau, PBM, is a leading regional competition law specialist whose practice covers antitrust litigation, international cartels and merger control. He is Co-Head of the Firm's Corporate & Commercial Department and Competition & Antitrust Practice.

He has successfully advised on a significant majority of Singapore's merger control cases, acted for the successful amnesty applicant of Singapore's first global cartel decision, the successful leniency applicant to its second one, and defended parties in 100% of Singapore's international cartel decisions to-date.

Daren has also worked on multiple landmark abuse of dominance cases to-date, including the first successful appeal to the Competition Appeal Board on liability.

E-mail: daren.shiau@allenandgledhill.com

Phone: 6890 7612

Sunit Chhabra is Head of the Firm's Tax Practice and specializes in tax and revenue law.

He has advised extensively on income tax, stamp duty and goods and services tax (GST) matters, including tax implications in relation to mergers and acquisitions, corporate restructurings, capital markets transactions and funds, and seeking advance rulings and/or clearances from the Inland Revenue Authority of Singapore (IRAS) in relation to proposed schemes or transactions to be undertaken.

Sunit also assists corporate and individual clients in replying to queries raised by IRAS, seeking resolution and settlement of disputes between them and IRAS and representing clients in tax hearings before the Board of Review and the appellate courts.

E-mail: sunit.chhabra@allenandgledhill.com

Phone: 6890 7735

Lim Pek Bur's principal areas of expertise are tax and wealth planning for ultra-high net worth clients.

Pek Bur has extensive experience in tax and stamp duty structuring, formulating defensive tax and stamp duty strategies and managing tax disputes with the tax authority, and has worked on large-scale mergers and acquisitions, initial public offerings of REITs, infrastructure projects, investment platforms, and joint ventures spanning various industries and different asset classes. Pek Bur also works with ultra-high net worth individuals on their bespoke wealth planning and philanthropic initiatives.

Pek Bur has been a Partner of Allen & Gledhill since 2006.

E-mail: lim.pekbur@allenandgledhill.com

Phone: 6890 7096

Yeo Boon Kiat regularly advises on a wide range of employment-related matters, such as employment contracts, handbooks and policies, employee incentive plans, collective bargaining and industrial relations, work passes, and the structuring of the transfer and termination of employment.

He also advises on a wide range of general corporate and commercial transactions, such as the procurement of goods and services (both public and private) and arrangements relating to agency and distributorship, manufacturing and outsourcing.

Boon Kiat is also familiar with the preparation and negotiation of project documentation for infrastructure and public-private partnership projects, particularly in the electricity, gas, telecommunications, media and transportation sectors. He has acted as project counsel for financiers, sponsors and developers in connection with such projects in Singapore and the region.

E-mail: yeo.boonkiat@allenandgledhill.com

Phone: 6890 7629

1 THE LEGAL ENVIRONMENT

[01] The Singapore legal system is a common law system, where case precedents and statutory provisions exist side by side. Singapore became an independent nation in 1965, and the Companies Act 1967 (the 'Companies Act') was passed in 1967. The Companies Act was based on the Malaysian model, which in turn was based on the Australian model at that time, which was itself derived from the then Companies Act of the United Kingdom. Over the years, the Companies Act has evolved uniquely from its predecessors. The takeover and corporate fund-raising provisions of the Companies Act were transposed to the Securities and Futures Act 2001 (SFA), which came into effect in 2002.

[02] The Companies Act continues to contain general corporate legislation, including provisions relating to the incorporation, management, administration and winding-up of companies. Two basic types of companies are provided for in the Companies Act, namely, the private company and the public company. A company is a private company where its constitution contains a restriction on the right to transfer shares and a limitation on the number of members to not more than fifty. A public company is a company that is not a private company. Public companies include companies limited by guarantee and companies limited by shares which are incorporated as public companies and which may or may not be listed on a stock exchange. Many public companies incorporated in Singapore are listed on the Singapore Exchange Securities Trading Limited (SGX-ST), and all Singapore-incorporated companies listed on the SGX-ST are necessarily public companies. The SGX-ST is currently the only securities exchange in Singapore.

[03] The law in this chapter is stated as of 1 May 2022.

2 BUSINESS VEHICLES

[04] This section provides a brief summary of the legal nature of the following business vehicles available in Singapore. Private companies are probably the most common form of business vehicle in Singapore while other forms of business vehicles are used where they better serve the commercial objectives of the parties depending on the objectives, the nature of the business activity, the funding for the business and other factors relevant to the stakeholders of the business.

[05] The various forms of business vehicles used for establishing a business presence in Singapore and the relevant statutes are:

(i) companies (private as well as public companies);
(ii) branches of foreign corporations;
(iii) representative offices;
(iv) sole proprietorships;
(v) partnerships;
(vi) limited partnerships (the LPs);
(vii) limited liability partnerships (the LLPs);

(viii) business trusts (the BTs); and
(ix) Variable capital companies (the VCCs).

Vehicle	*Governing Statute on Incorporation/Registration*
Companies	Companies Act 1967
Branches of foreign corporations	Companies Act 1967
Representative offices	Guidelines issued by Enterprise Singapore
Sole proprietorships	Business Names Registration Act 2014
Partnerships	Business Names Registration Act 2014
LPs	Limited Partnerships Act 2008
LLPs	Limited Liability Partnerships Act 2005
BTs	Business Trusts Act 2004
VCCs	Variable Capital Companies Act 2018

[06] The principal regulator of corporate entities and businesses in Singapore is the Accounting and Corporate Regulatory Authority (ACRA). Under the ACRA, the Registrar of Companies administers the Companies Act, the Registrar of Business Names administers the Business Names Registration Act 2014, the Registrar of Limited Liability Partnerships administers the Limited Liability Partnerships Act 2005 (LLP Act), the Registrar of Limited Partnerships administers the Limited Partnerships Act (LP Act), and the Registrar of Variable Capital Companies administers the Variable Capital Companies Act 2018 (the VCC Act).

2.1 Sole Proprietorship and Partnership

[07] The term 'sole proprietorship' is used to describe a person who engages in business on his own without being associated with others. A 'partnership' consists of two or more persons carrying on business in common with a view to profit.

[08] Both sole proprietorships and partnerships are not separate legal entities. The owner of a sole proprietorship is personally liable to creditors of the sole proprietorship for all debts and liabilities incurred in the name of the business without limit. Similarly, each partner of a partnership is jointly liable with the other partners in respect of all debts and liabilities of the partnership incurred during his participation in the partnership.

[09] A partnership may not be made up of more than twenty persons. This restriction on the size of a partnership, however, does not apply to one that is formed for the purpose of carrying on any professional services like a partnership formed to practice law, medicine, accounting, etc.

2.2 Limited Partnership

[10] LPs are commonly used in businesses focusing on single or limited-term projects, as well as for situations where one or more financial backers or investors do not wish to take up an active role in the management of the business, preferring to entrust its management to one or more persons who are willing to assume liability for the debts and liabilities of the business.

[11] LPs are regulated by the LP Act, the Partnership Act 1890 (where not inconsistent with the provisions of the LP Act) and the rules of equity and common law applicable to partnerships (where not inconsistent with the express provisions of the Partnership Act 1890). The LP framework is administered by the ACRA.

[12] An LP is not a legal entity and does not have a separate legal personality. As such, it can neither own property under its own name nor can it sue or be sued in its own name. Like a partnership, an LP is a relationship which subsists between persons carrying on business in common with a view to profit.

[13] An LP must consist of at least one limited partner and at least one general partner. Limited partners and general partners may be either individuals or corporations (which need not be incorporated in Singapore). A general partner is liable for all debts and obligations of the LP incurred while it is a general partner of the LP. A limited partner, however, will not be liable for the debts and obligations of the LP beyond the amount of its agreed contribution subject to the provisions of the LP Act. In particular, to enjoy limited liability, limited partners may not take part in the management of the LP and must be registered as a limited partner of the LP under the LP Act. Limited partners do not have the power to bind an LP.

2.3 Limited Liability Partnership

[14] An LLP may be used by any two or more persons associated for carrying on a lawful business with a view to profit. An LLP is essentially a partnership with limited liability. However, unlike a partnership, an LLP is a body corporate with a legal personality separate from that of its partners. An LLP's obligation is solely that of the LLP. The law relating to partnerships does not apply to an LLP except as otherwise provided by the LLP Act.

[15] A partner of an LLP is not personally liable for the wrongful act or omission of any other partner of the LLP but is personally liable in tort for his own wrongful act or omission. Where one of the partners of the LLP is liable to any person as a result

of his own wrongful act or omission that was committed in the course of the business of the LLP or with the LLP's authority, the LLP is liable to the same extent as the partner. The liabilities of the LLP are met out of the property of the LLP.

[16] An LLP must be made up of at least two partners and must have at least one manager who is a natural person of full age and capacity and who is ordinarily resident in Singapore. Every LLP must have a registered office within Singapore to which all communications and notices may be addressed.

2.4 Business Trust

[17] Business trusts (BTs) are business enterprises set up as trust structures and are created by the execution of a trust deed like any other trust. BTs are governed by the rules of common law and equally under the Trustees Act. However, the Trustees Act 1967 does not apply to a registered BT, which is subject to the s Business Trusts Act 2004. The s Business Trusts Act 2004 regulates the corporate governance of registered BTs.

[18] A BT differs from a company in that it is not a legal entity. It is created by a trust deed under which an entity named the trustee-manager has legal ownership of the assets of the business enterprise and manages the business for the benefit of the beneficiaries of the trust. Subject to the trust deed of a BT, a trustee-manager may, however, appoint agents to carry out and perform its functions. BTs also differ from other traditional trusts, such as a private family trust or a unit trust, as they actively undertake business operations.

[19] Investors of a BT take a stake in the underlying business by purchasing units in the BT. Unitholders in the BTs, being beneficiaries of the trust, hold beneficial interests in the assets of the BT. A unitholder of a registered BT is not liable to contribute to the registered BT or in respect of any debts, liabilities or obligations incurred by the trustee-manager in its capacity as trustee-manager for the registered BT. The liability of a unitholder of a registered BT is limited to the amount of money that he has expressly agreed to contribute to the registered BT.

2.5 Companies

[20] A company is legally a person separate and distinct from its members. Flowing from this independent legal personality of a company, the members of the company are not liable to creditors of the company for debts and liabilities incurred by the company. A company is responsible for its own debts and liabilities. The members of a company cannot be sued for the debts of the company.

[21] Subject to the constitution of a company, management of the company is vested in the board of directors, whereas the day-to-day running of the company will usually fall to the managing director or the chief executive officer.

2.6 Liability of Members of Company

[22] The liability of the members of a company to contribute to the assets of the company upon its liquidation may be limited or unlimited. In an unlimited company, the liability of the members is without limitation. In a limited company, the liability of the members depends on whether the company is limited by shares or by guarantee.

[23] A member of a company limited by shares may be called upon to pay any amount remaining unpaid on his shares to the company in discharge of his liability not only upon the liquidation of the company but also at any time during the existence of the company. The liability of the members of a company limited by shares is limited to the amount remaining unpaid on their shares. There are no minimum capitalization requirements under Singapore law except that at least one share must be issued upon incorporation.

[24] A member of a company limited by guarantee may be called upon to discharge his liability to contribute to the assets of the company only in the event of the liquidation of the company. The liability of the members of a company limited by guarantee is limited to the amount which they have agreed to contribute. Therefore, a company limited by a guarantee does not obtain its initial working capital from its members. In contrast, the company limited by shares can obtain its initial working capital by issuing shares to its members which are paid for by the members.

2.7 Private Company Versus Public Company

[25] A company having a share capital is a private company:

(i) where the right to transfer shares is restricted; and
(ii) where the number of shareholders is restricted by its constitution to fifty (counting joint holders of shares as one, and excluding current employees of the company or its subsidiaries and former employees of the company or its subsidiaries who became members when they were employed by the company).

[26] A public company has been defined as one other than a private company. Essentially, it is a company where the number of shareholders can be more than fifty. Generally, a public company is subject to more regulation than a private company.

[27] Previously, only public companies could raise capital by offering shares and debentures to the public. With effect from 1 April 2004, private companies are no longer prohibited from offering shares and debentures to the public, thereby removing what had been a fundamental difference between private and public companies. Where shares in or debentures of a company are offered to the public, a prospectus which complies with the relevant provisions of the SFA must be issued.

2.8 Exempt Private Company

[28] Private companies may further be classified into exempt private companies and non-exempt private companies.

[29] An exempt private company must be a private company:

(i) in which no beneficial interest in the shares of the company is held directly or indirectly by a corporation and which has no more than twenty members; or
(ii) that is wholly owned by the government, which the Minister, in the national interest, declares by notification in the Gazette to be an exempt private company.

[30] Exempt private companies are exempt from the prohibition in section 162 of the Companies Act against a company extending loans or quasi-loans to, or entering into credit transactions or related arrangements with, its directors or directors of its related corporations and the prohibition in section 163 of the Companies Act against a company extending loans or quasi-loans to, or entering into credit transactions with, another company or limited liability partnership in which a director of the first-mentioned company has an interest of 20% or more.

2.9 Branch of Foreign Corporation

[31] This form of business organization is only available to foreign corporations. The obligation to register is imposed on all foreign corporations which have a place of business or which carry on business in Singapore.

[32] Under the Companies Act, every registered branch of a foreign corporation in Singapore must:

(i) appoint at least one natural person ordinarily resident in Singapore who is authorized to accept on its behalf service of process and any notices required to be served on the corporation;
(ii) have a registered office in Singapore; and
(iii) lodge:
  (a) financial statements made up to the end of its last financial year together with a declaration in the prescribed form verifying that the copies are true copies of the documents so required and, in the case where the financial statements are audited, a statement of the name of the auditor;
  (b) a duly audited statement showing its assets used in and liabilities arising out of its operations in Singapore as at the date to which its balance sheet was made up;
  (c) a duly audited profit and loss account which, in so far as is practicable, complies with the requirements of the accounting standards made or formulated by the Accounting Standards Council of Singapore and

which gives a true and fair view of the profit or loss arising out of the company's operation in Singapore for the last preceding financial year of the company; and

(d) a statement of the name of the auditor who audited the documents listed in (b) and (c), with the Registrar of Companies, within sixty days of its Annual General Meeting (AGM) if the foreign corporation is required by the law of its place of incorporation or formation to table financial statements at its AGM, or, in any other case, within such period as the directors of the foreign corporation would have been required to lodge its financial statements if the foreign corporation was a public company incorporated under the Companies Act which does not keep a branch register outside Singapore (subject to certain conditions under the Companies Act).

2.10 Representative Office

[33] Another method by which a foreign corporation may establish a presence in Singapore is to set up a representative office. However, the activities that may be engaged by a representative office must be confined to conducting market research and feasibility studies. A representative office is merely an administrative creature and has no legal status.

[34] A representative office of a foreign commercial entity may operate in Singapore for a maximum of three years from its commencement date, provided that the representative office status is evaluated and renewed. Representative offices which decide to continue their presence in Singapore thereafter should register their operations with the ACRA.

2.11 Variable Capital Company

[35] The VCC is a corporate entity incorporated under the VCC Act instead of the Companies Act. Once established, the VCC's operations are governed by the VCC Act and its subsidiary legislation, parts of it which apply provisions of the CA with or without modifications. A VCC must be managed by a fund manager in compliance with the regulations of the Monetary Authority of Singapore (MAS).

[36] A VCC has a separate legal identity from its shareholders. As such, it can hold property under its own name and can sue or be sued in its own name. The rights and obligations of a VCC are separate from those of its shareholders and directors. A VCC can have several sub-funds, each with segregated assets and liabilities ('umbrella VCC'). A sub-fund under an umbrella VCC is not a separate legal entity. However, an umbrella VCC can sue or be sued in respect of its sub-funds as if each sub-fund were a separate legal person and the property of a sub-fund is subject to orders of a court as it would have been if the sub-fund were a separate legal person.

[37] A VCC is managed by its board of directors. A VCC must have at least one director. Where a VCC has only one director, the director must be ordinarily resident in Singapore and be either a director or a qualified representative of the manager of the VCC. Where a VCC has more than one director, at least one of the directors must be ordinarily resident in Singapore, and at least one director (who may be the same director as the one ordinarily resident in Singapore) must be either a director or a qualified representative of the manager of the VCC. A director of a VCC must be a natural person who has attained the age of 18 years and who is of full legal capacity. If the VCC comprises at least one authorized scheme (i.e., the scheme has been authorized by the MAS and units in the scheme may be offered to the public), the provisions of the Code on Collective Investment Schemes issued by the MAS (including on the appointment of VCC directors) will apply.

[38] A VCC has a variable capital structure that provides flexibility in the issuance and redemption of its shares. The VCC Act provides that the provision for shares in a VCC to be issued, redeemed or repurchased at a price equal to the proportion of the net asset value (NAV) of the VCC represented by each share will be implied in the constitution of every VCC, subject to any adjustments for fees and charges in accordance with the VCC's constitution. A VCC may also issue different classes of shares with different rights and dividend payment policies, although the rights attached to each share must be set out in the VCC's constitution.

3 COMPLIANCE REQUIREMENTS OF A COMPANY

[39] The following are some of the key compliance and reporting requirements in respect of a company which is the common form of business vehicle in Singapore:

(i) Every company incorporated in Singapore must have at least one director who is ordinarily resident in Singapore and at least one company secretary whose principal or only place of residence is Singapore and who is not debarred under section 155B of the Companies Act from acting as secretary of the company. The director must be at least 18 years old and of full legal capacity. The company secretary should be appointed within six months of incorporation.

(ii) Each company incorporated in Singapore must have a registered office from the date of incorporation at which service of processes and notices can be effected. The office must be open and accessible to the public for at least three hours during ordinary business hours on each business day.

(iii) Auditors have to be appointed within three months from the date of incorporation of the company. Except for certain dormant companies and 'small companies' (as defined in the Thirteenth Schedule to the Companies Act), a company's accounts must be audited once a year.

(iv) Each company incorporated in Singapore must prepare their annual financial accounts in accordance with the accounting standards made or formulated by the Accounting Standards Council of Singapore.

(v) Each company incorporated in Singapore must hold an AGM after the end of each financial year within: (a) four months in the case of a public company that is listed; or (b) six months in the case of any other company, except as otherwise permitted under the Companies Act. Private companies may, however, dispense with AGMs if, at a general meeting of the company, a resolution to that effect is passed by all members entitled to vote at the meeting. In addition, a private company need not hold an AGM for a financial year if at the end of that financial year: (a) it is a private company and has sent to all persons entitled to receive notice of general meetings of the company the financial statements (or in the case of a parent company, a copy of the consolidated financial statements and balance sheet (including every document required by law to be attached thereto) which is duly audited, not later than five months after the end of the financial year to which the financial statements, or consolidated financial statements and balance sheet, relate; or (b) it is both a private company and a dormant relevant company the directors of which are, under section 201A of the Companies Act, exempt from the requirements of section 201 of the Companies Act for the financial year.

(vi) Each company incorporated in Singapore must file its Annual Return with the ACRA: (a) in the case of a company having a share capital and keeping a branch register in any place outside Singapore, within six months are the end of its financial year for listed companies, and in any other case, within eight months after the end of its financial year; and (b) in any other case, within five months after the end of its financial year for listed companies, and in any other case, within seven months after the end of its financial year.

4 LAWS AFFECTING M&A

4.1 Companies Act 1967

[40] The Companies Act is also relevant to corporate acquisitions and mergers. Section 210 of the Companies Act provides for schemes of arrangement. Singapore-incorporated companies may also use the amalgamation process in sections 215A–215K of the Companies Act to facilitate the combination of such companies. Section 215 of the Companies Act governs the compulsory acquisition of the shares of minority shareholders once an offeror has acquired 90% of the target's shares through a takeover offer (excluding the shares held by the offeror, its related corporations[1] and their respective nominees). Developments pertaining to section 215 include the coming into force of the Companies (Amendment) Act 2014, which amended the Companies Act in two phases. Some amendments took effect on 1 July 2015 while most of the remaining amendments came into effect on

[1] Under the Companies Act, a related corporation is a subsidiary, holding company or a fellow subsidiary.

3 January 2016. With effect from 3 January 2016, 'shares' referred to in section 215 of the Companies Act include units of shares (e.g., options and convertibles). In addition, with effect from 3 January 2016, the operation of section 215 has been extended to cover individual offerors. Previously, section 215 only applied to offerors which were companies.

[41] The Companies Act contains provisions relating to financial assistance in sections 76 and 76A. The financial assistance provisions restrict a public company incorporated in Singapore or a company incorporated in Singapore whose holding company or ultimate holding company is a public company, from providing financial assistance, whether directly or indirectly, to any person in the acquisition or proposed acquisition of shares or units of shares in that company or the holding company or ultimate holding company of that company. The provisions relating to financial assistance are widely drafted. For instance, if a party seeking to acquire shares in a target company procures the target company to charge its assets to refinance a loan taken by the offeror to acquire the target company, this may constitute financial assistance by the target company. The prohibition against financial assistance for private companies has been removed with effect from 1 July 2015.

[42] Financial assistance is a restricted but not a prohibited activity under the Companies Act. It is possible to 'whitewash' financial assistance, where the company obtains its shareholders' approval by a special resolution and complies with the procedures set out in section 76(9A)–76(14) of the Companies Act, which include the filing of certain prescribed forms with the Registrar of Companies (the 'Registrar'), publishing a notice of intention to give financial assistance in a daily newspaper and permitting objections to be made by shareholders, debenture-holders, creditors and the Registrar. To address concerns that the financial assistance restricted or rendered more expensive a range of potentially beneficial or innocuous transactions, certain new exceptions to the financial assistance prohibitions for a public company or a subsidiary of a public company were introduced in July 2015. In particular, the most commonly used exemption is set out in section 76(9BA) of the Companies Act, which allows a public company or a subsidiary of a public company to provide financial assistance where the giving of the assistance does not materially prejudice interests of the company or its shareholders or the company's ability to pay its creditors. This exemption can be relied on by a company if its board of directors passes a resolution that (i) the company should provide such assistance; and (ii) the terms and conditions under which the assistance is proposed to be given are fair and reasonable to the company, setting out in full the grounds for the directors' conclusions, and such resolution is lodged with the Registrar.

4.2 Securities and Futures Act 2001

[43] Part VIII of the SFA contains legislative provisions relating to takeover offers made for public companies in three sections. Section 138 of the SFA provides for the establishment of the Securities Industry Council (SIC). The SIC is the principal regulator which oversees the Singapore Code on Take-overs and Mergers (the 'Take-over Code'). Section 139 provides that the MAS has the power, on the advice of the SIC, to issue the Take-over Code, and to make amendments to the Take-over Code from time to time. Section 140 lists the offences relating to takeover offers. It is an offence for a person to give notice or publicly announce that he intends to make a takeover offer if he has no intention to make one. It is also an offence to make a takeover offer if a person has no reasonable or probable grounds for believing that he will be able to perform his obligations pursuant to the offer being accepted or approved.

4.3 Take-Over Code and the SIC

[44] The Take-over Code applies to the acquisition of voting control of public companies. It applies to corporations (including corporations not incorporated under Singapore law) with a primary listing of their equity securities, and registered BTs or Real Estate Investment Trusts (REITs) with a primary listing of their units, in Singapore. While the Take-over Code was drafted with listed public companies, listed registered BTs and REITs in mind, unlisted public companies and unlisted registered BTs or REITs with more than fifty shareholders or unitholders, as the case may be, and net tangible assets of SGD5 m or more must also observe, wherever possible and appropriate, the letter and spirit of the Take-over Code as set out in its General Principles and Rules. The Take-over Code does not apply to take-overs or mergers of other unlisted public companies or unlisted BTs, or private companies. With respect to foreign-incorporated companies and foreign-registered BTs, the Take-over Code applies, prima facie, only to those with a primary listing in Singapore.

[45] The Take-over Code applies to all offerors, whether they are natural persons or not, be they resident in Singapore or not and whether citizens of Singapore or not, and whether they are corporations or bodies unincorporated, be they incorporated or carrying on business in Singapore or not. The Take-over Code also extends to acts done or omitted both in and outside Singapore.

[46] The Take-over Code is administered and enforced by the SIC. The SIC is provided with discretion to waive the application of the Take-over Code in relation to corporations and BTs with a primary listing in Singapore, public companies and registered BTs with a primary listing overseas, and unlisted public companies and unlisted registered BTs with more than fifty shareholders or unitholders, as the case may be, and net tangible assets of SGD5 m or more.

[47] The SIC is made up of representatives from the government, the MAS and the private sector. The day-to-day business of the SIC is conducted by a professionally staffed full-time Secretariat. The MAS is a statutory board formed under the Monetary Authority of Singapore Act 1970 and is the de facto central bank of Singapore, as well as the integrated regulator of the banking, insurance, financial, securities and futures industries.

[48] The Take-over Code contains General Principles, Rules and Notes and is supplemented by Practice Statements issued by the SIC from time to time. Nonetheless, the Take-over Code notes that it is impracticable to devise rules in sufficient detail to cover all circumstances that can arise in takeover and merger transactions. Therefore, both the letter and spirit of the Take-over Code must be observed, especially in the circumstances not explicitly covered by any Rules. The SIC may, pursuant to section 139 of the SFA, also issue rulings on the interpretation of the General Principles and the Rules in the Take-over Code and lay down the practices to be followed by the parties in a takeover offer or a matter connected therewith. In the course of a takeover, it is not unusual to require rulings from the SIC. The SFA provides that such rulings or practices issued by the SIC are final and cannot be challenged in any court.

[49] The SIC is available for a confidential consultation on points of interpretation of the Take-over Code. When there is any doubt as to whether a proposed course of conduct in a takeover offer accords with the General Principles or Rules of the Take-over Code, it is advisable for the parties or their advisers to consult the SIC in advance, as such confidential consultation minimizes the risk of breaches of the Take-over Code.

[50] The parties to a takeover are primarily responsible for ensuring observance of the provisions of the Take-over Code. If there appears to be a breach of the Take-over Code, the SIC may summon the alleged offenders to appear before the SIC for a hearing where every alleged offender will have the opportunity to answer allegations and also to call witnesses. The SFA provides the SIC with powers to investigate any acts of misconduct in relation to or connected with a transaction involving a takeover or merger transaction, where it has reason to believe that any party or any financial adviser is in breach of the Take-over Code. In this respect, the SIC is empowered to make enquiries, summon persons to give evidence on oath or affirmation, or produce any document or material necessary for the purpose of the enquiry.

[51] Although the Take-over Code does not have the force of law and does not give rise to criminal proceedings, its breach may result in the imposition of sanctions by the SIC. Sanctions, which the SIC may impose, include private reprimands, public censure and, where the breach is flagrant, further action as the SIC thinks fit, including actions designed to deprive the offender temporarily or permanently of its ability to enjoy the facilities of the securities market. In the case of advisers, the SIC may also require such advisers to abstain from taking on Take-over Code-related work for a stated period. Where a person has breached the Take-over Code, the SIC may also make a ruling requiring the person concerned to pay holders or former holders of securities in the offeree company such amount as it thinks just and reasonable to ensure that holders receive what they would have been entitled to receive had the relevant rule been complied with. The SIC may also rule that interest be paid on the sums.

[52] If the SIC finds evidence to show that a criminal offence has been committed under the Companies Act, the SFA or any relevant criminal law, it will refer the matter to the appropriate authority. It is noted that the SFA sets out the criminal

offence of insider trading and prohibits a person with non-public price-sensitive information from dealing in the shares of a target company.

[53] The Take-over Code was last updated in January 2019. Among other changes, the Take-over Code was amended to clarify its application to companies with a dual-class share structure that are primarily listed on the SGX-ST.

4.4 Stock Exchange Rules

[54] Where either the acquiring company or the target company is a company listed on the SGX-ST, the SGX-ST Listing Manual (the 'Listing Manual') also applies. In summary, the Listing Manual contains rules regulating the general affairs of listed companies, and therefore, its provisions have to be taken into account if either the acquiring company or the target company is listed on the SGX-ST.

[55] The listing rules set out in the Listing Manual do not have statutory force. They are issued by the SGX-ST, subject to the approval of the MAS as required under the SFA. The SFA also empowers the SGX-ST to apply to a court for an order to enforce compliance with the listing rules, though this power has been rarely, if ever, used. In practice, ready observance of the Listing Manual is advised as failure to comply may result in sanctions being imposed by the SGX-ST, ranging from a public reprimand to a delisting. Furthermore, the SFA provides that a company listed on the SGX-ST must not intentionally, recklessly or negligently fail to notify the SGX-ST of information on specified events or matters, as they occur or arise, which are required to be disclosed under the listing rules for the purpose of making information available to the market.

[56] The Listing Manual sets out the continuing listing requirements and corporate disclosure policy which a listed company has to comply with. A listed company is required to keep the SGX-ST, its shareholders and other holders of its listed securities informed of all material information relating to it, and this includes information in relation to a takeover, merger or acquisition.

[57] A listed company intending to make an acquisition or a listed company which is the target of an offer will have to make the necessary disclosures in a timely manner. The information to be disclosed has to be factual, clear and succinct, and contain sufficient quantitative information to allow investors to evaluate its relative importance to the activities of the listed company. This includes information pertaining to the particulars of the transaction, its rationale, any consideration payable, any analysis of financial impact, the conditions for the transaction and the disclosure of any conflicts of interest.

[58] The Listing Manual is also relevant where a listed offeror offers new shares as consideration in its takeover offer. Where the target company is a listed company, the Listing Manual contains provisions relating to reverse takeovers. The approval of the SGX-ST is required in a reverse takeover for the transaction itself as well as for the listing of new shares in the target company.

4.5 Competition Act 2004

[59] In Singapore, the merger control regime is prescribed under the Competition Act 2004 (the 'Competition Act'). The Competition Act is the principal statute governing the competition law regime in Singapore. Merger control provisions under the Competition Act came into force on 1 July 2007. Merger controls are dealt with under 'Competition Aspects' below.

4.6 Statutory Shareholding Restrictions in Specific Industries

[60] Other statutes relating to particular industries also govern takeover activity in Singapore insofar as they limit or require prior regulatory approval for share ownership in companies engaged in those industries. Those industries are generally industries perceived to be critical to national interests, for instance, banking, finance, insurance and media.

[61] Examples of such statutes include the Banking Act 1970, Finance Companies Act 1967, Insurance Act 1966 and Newspaper and Printing Presses Act 1974.

5 METHODS OF TAKEOVER

5.1 Public Offers

[62] A takeover or acquisition of shares may be effected in various ways, taking into account financing preferences, tax considerations and market conditions. The most efficient method for any particular transaction depends on the circumstances and the objectives of the transaction parties. The main methods, which will be discussed in further detail, are cash purchases and/or share swaps, reverse takeovers and schemes of arrangement. The amalgamation process, as set out in section 215A–215K of the Companies Act, may also be used, although this approach is less common in practice.

[63] The end result of these various takeover methods is that the target company becomes a subsidiary of the acquiring company. This enables the acquiring company to consolidate the results of the target company with its own. Apart from the above methods, there are other ways to achieve this result, for instance, incorporating a new holding company to acquire both the acquirer and the target company or amalgamating the target company into the acquirer so that the target company ceases to exist as a legal entity.

5.2 Cash Purchase and/or Share Swap

[64] An acquiring entity may offer cash, shares or other securities or a mixture of any of these as consideration for the takeover bid. The offer may be in the form of cash from the acquirer's own resources, debt financing or an underwritten issue of the acquirer's own shares. In a cash purchase, the acquiring entity makes an offer and acquires the shares of the target company for cash only. In a share swap arrangement, the acquiring entity acquires shares in the target company from the shareholders of the target company and, in return, issues its shares as consideration.

[65] The Take-over Code provides that a mandatory offer has to be in the form of a cash offer or be accompanied by a cash alternative. In the case of a voluntary offer, a cash offer or an offer accompanied by a cash alternative has to be made in certain circumstances (*see* the discussion of mandatory offers and voluntary offers in paragraphs [86]–[97] below). Apart from any mandatory cash and securities components stipulated in the Take-over Code, the choice of consideration for the takeover offer will depend, among other things, upon the acquirer's own financial position and, if it is proposing an underwritten share issue to effect a share swap, the market's appetite for its shares. In addition, the voluntary delisting regime under the Listing Manual requires takeover offers to offer a cash alternative, save where the acquirer is exercising its right of compulsory acquisition.

The shareholders of a target company may be given a choice of consideration, for example, cash with a partial share alternative. They may also be offered the facility to be able to mix and match different forms of consideration by making certain elections to the acquirer, provided that all shareholders of the target company are treated fairly and equally. In a Take-over Bulletin published by the SIC in September 2019, the SIC noted a recent takeover offer via a scheme of arrangement which proposed to allow target shareholders to elect to receive either cash or securities consideration (but not a mixture at both) in respect of the shares held in their securities accounts. This would mean that target shareholders who are able to open different securities accounts would be able to elect to receive shares for some of their target shares, and cash for some of their target shares, and one of the major undertaking shareholders would be electing to receive different forms of consideration under this arrangement. The SIC was of the view that, notwithstanding that the other target shareholders could similarly set up separate securities accounts to receive both cash and securities consideration, it was not appropriate for the target shareholders to have to take this step in order to receive the same treatment as the major undertaking shareholder. The SIC noted that the offeror, in the implementation of its rules for the election of consideration, should ensure that all target shareholders are treated fairly and equally without them having to take additional steps.

5.3 Reverse Takeovers

[66] In a reverse takeover transaction, the acquirer transfers to the target company certain assets and business in exchange for new shares in the target company. The acquirer may then be required to make or may decide to make a takeover offer for all the remaining shares in the target company that it does not own. Where the target company is a listed company, the effect of a reverse takeover is that the acquirer gains control of a listed company, and such transactions are also known as 'back door' listings. These transactions are subject to additional approvals and requirements by the SGX-ST.

[67] The Listing Manual contains specific provisions defining and regulating 'very substantial acquisitions or reverse takeovers'. Whether a transaction is considered a very substantial acquisition or a reverse takeover depends on various formulas set out in the Listing Manual or whether a transaction would result in a change in control of the listed company. In calculating whether or not a transaction is a very substantial acquisition for the purposes of the Listing Manual, the following figures are taken into account: the net profits attributable to the assets acquired or disposed of, compared with the group's net profits; the aggregate value of the consideration given or received, compared with the market capitalization of the target company based on the total number of issued shares excluding treasury shares; or the number of equity securities issued by the target company as consideration for an acquisition, compared with the number of equity securities previously in issue. If any one of the relative figures is 100% or more, or is one which will result in a change in control of the issuer, the transaction will be regarded as a very substantial acquisition or reverse takeover, respectively. The Listing Manual requires the transaction to be made conditional upon the approval of shareholders. The shareholders' circular for a meeting held to seek the shareholders' approval is required to contain specific information prescribed in the Listing Manual. In addition, in a reverse takeover, the shareholders will have to approve the issue of new shares in accordance with the Companies Act.

[68] Furthermore, in a reverse takeover, the transaction, as well as the issue and listing of the new shares, will have to be approved by the SGX-ST. In this respect, the SGX-ST requires that the enlarged group consisting of the offeror and offered companies will have to comply with the SGX-ST's listing requirements. 'Back door' listings are viewed by the SGX-ST in the same way as initial public offerings.

5.4 Scheme of Arrangement

[69] Instead of making a takeover offer, an acquisition of a public company may also be effected by a scheme of arrangement under section 210 of the Companies Act. In a scheme of arrangement, the target company cancels its existing shares and issues new shares in the target company to the acquirer, in consideration of the acquirer paying cash or issuing new shares in the acquiring company to the shareholders of the target company, or a combination of both cash and shares. Alternatively, outstanding shares in the target company may be transferred from the shareholders of the target company to the acquirer. As a section 210 scheme of arrangement is an arrangement between a company and its members, only the target company may initiate a scheme of arrangement. It is, therefore, not typically available as an option in a hostile acquisition. A scheme of arrangement will usually be used only in a situation where the acquirer wishes to acquire all the shares of a target company, and such acquisition is 'welcomed' by the target company.

[70] All schemes of arrangement are subject to compliance with the Take-over Code. However, the SIC may, subject to conditions, exempt a scheme from certain provisions of the Take-over Code. These provisions include those relating to the offer timetable and terms of the offer. The SIC will normally grant such exemptions if the following conditions are met. First, the acquirer and its concert parties as well as common substantial shareholders of the scheme companies (*see* paragraph [71] for an explanation of who is a substantial shareholder) are to abstain from voting on the scheme. Second, persons and their concert parties who, as a result of the scheme, would acquire 30% or more in a scheme company or a new entity that holds the scheme company or companies, or persons who, as a result of the scheme (if they already hold 30%–50% before the scheme), would increase their voting rights by more than 1% in any period of six months, are to abstain from voting on the scheme. Third, the directors of a scheme company who are also directors of the other scheme company or who are acting in concert with those persons mentioned in the earlier conditions are to abstain from making a recommendation on the scheme to the shareholders of the scheme companies. Fourth, the scheme company which is, in effect, the target company has to appoint an Independent Financial Adviser (IFA) to advise its shareholders on the scheme of arrangement. Where the scheme of arrangement involves a reverse takeover or a 'merger of equals', each of the scheme companies must appoint an IFA to advise their respective shareholders. In cases of doubt, the SIC should be consulted.

[71] Various other approvals are also required for a scheme of arrangement to take effect. In accordance with section 210 of the Companies Act, a scheme of arrangement requires the approval of a majority in number of members of the target company present and voting in person or by proxy, representing at least 75% in value of the shares voted at a scheme meeting. In the voting process, the acquirer and its related parties, as well as common substantial shareholders of the acquirer and the target company, would have to abstain from voting. A substantial shareholder is one who has an 'interest' (as defined by the SFA) of 5% or more of the total votes attached to all the voting shares in a company (*see* paragraph [81] for elaboration). Furthermore, in accordance with the Companies Act, the scheme also requires the sanction of the Singapore High Court (the 'High Court'). Once an order for a scheme of arrangement has been approved by the High Court, it binds all shareholders, including those who had objected to it at the scheme meeting or before the High Court. Following amendments introduced by the Companies (Amendment) Act 2014 which came into effect on 3 January 2016, the company is now allowed to enter into schemes of arrangement with holders of units of shares (e.g., options and convertibles), and the High Court has the discretion to approve a scheme even if the scheme does not have the requisite approval at the scheme meeting. The latter amendment was aimed at preventing the defeat of a member's scheme of arrangement by opposing parties engaged in share-splitting, which involves one or more members transferring small parcels of shares to a large number of other persons who are willing to vote in accordance with the transferors' instructions.

[72] In a scheme of arrangement, the target company will issue a scheme document to its shareholders. Essentially, the scheme document is a circular to convene, at the direction of the High Court, a meeting of the shareholders of the target company to approve the scheme of arrangement and which also contains an explanatory statement to explain to shareholders the effect of the implementation of the scheme. In order to satisfy the conditions (set out in paragraph [70]) for an exemption from selected provisions of the Take-over Code, the scheme document must disclose the names of those common substantial shareholders, and persons who would acquire more voting rights as a result of the scheme, who are required to abstain from voting. The scheme document must also disclose their voting rights in the scheme company and/or the new entity after the scheme of arrangement, and furthermore state that by voting for the scheme, shareholders are agreeing to the person acquiring or consolidating effective control without having to make a general offer under the Take-over Code.

[73] On 3 October 2008, the SIC issued a Practice Statement on 'Trust Schemes in respect of Mergers and Privatizations' (the 'Practice Statement'). A trust scheme may effect a merger or privatization of a BT or REIT via an amendment to the trust deed to include provisions allowing a specific merger or privatization to take place. Such trust schemes are subject to unitholder approval. The provisions of the Take-over Code apply to these trust schemes, but the SIC may exempt a trust scheme from complying with some of these conditions. Given that dissenting unitholders of a BT or REIT will lose their units compulsorily once such trust scheme is approved, the SIC states in the Practice Statement that it is concerned that the trust scheme should be fair and reasonable. The Practice Statement sets out the conditions that must be fulfilled by a trust scheme before the SIC would consider exempting the trust scheme from certain specific provisions of the Take-over Code. These conditions are now set out in the Take-over Code.

It should also be noted that recent changes to the Listing Manual have clarified that the requirements to provide a reasonable exit alternative on the delisting of a company will apply in respect of a takeover by way of a scheme of arrangement ('Exit Offer'). Under such requirements, an Exit Offer must be fair and reasonable and must include a cash alternative as a default alternative.

5.5 Amalgamation Process

[74] Acquisition of a public company may also be effected through an amalgamation process. Such a process may involve either two or more companies amalgamating and continuing as one company or two or more companies amalgamating and forming a new company. The amalgamation process does not involve the sanction of the High Court, unlike in a scheme of arrangement.

[75] The clearance of the SIC is required for an exemption from certain provisions of the Take-over Code. These provisions include those relating to the offer timetable and the terms of the offer. Under the Take-over Code, the application would normally be granted by the SIC if the conditions set out in paragraph [70], which are also applicable to schemes of arrangement, are met. Additionally, the SIC would require the amalgamation proposal to be posted within thirty-five days of the announcement of the amalgamation, and for the amalgamation to be effective by 5.30 p.m. on the sixtieth day after the date of posting the amalgamation proposal.

[76] In respect of a full amalgamation process (being the method applicable to public companies), the following approvals, as provided for in section 215C of the Companies Act, are required:

- (i) an amalgamation proposal, containing the information required by the Companies Act, must be approved by the members of each amalgamating company by special resolution at a general meeting and by any third party if so provided for in the amalgamation proposal;
- (ii) the board of directors of each amalgamating company, before the general meeting, has:
  - (a) resolved that the amalgamation is in the best interest of the amalgamating company;
  - (b) made a solvency statement in relation to the amalgamating company (relating to its ability to pay its debts as they fall due as at the date of the statement and the value of its assets not being less than the value of its liabilities, including contingent liabilities) in accordance with section 215I of the Companies Act; and
  - (c) made a solvency statement in relation to the amalgamated company (relating to its ability to pay its debts as they fall due as at the effective date of the amalgamation and the value of its assets not being less than the value of its liabilities, including contingent liabilities) in accordance with section 215J the Companies Act;

    The requirement for directors of an amalgamating company to provide solvency statements in respect of such company, as well as the other amalgamating company, may be one of the reasons why the amalgamation process is less commonly used for takeovers in Singapore.
- (iii) each director who votes in favour of the resolution and the making of the solvency statements described in subparagraph (ii)(b) above has signed a declaration stating that certain specified conditions set out in the Companies Act are satisfied and the grounds of that opinion;

(iv) the board of directors of each amalgamating company has sent to every member of the amalgamating company, not less than twenty-one days before the general meeting, *inter alia*, a copy of the amalgamation proposal, the declaration of the directors set out in subparagraph (iii) above, a statement of any material interests of the directors and such further information and explanation as may be necessary to enable a reasonable member of the amalgamating company to understand the nature and implications, for the amalgamating company and its members, of the proposed amalgamation; and

(v) the directors of each amalgamating company have, not less than twenty-one days before the general meeting, sent a copy of the amalgamation proposal to every secured creditor of the amalgamating company as well as published in at least one daily English newspaper a notice of the proposed amalgamation.

[77] In order to effect the amalgamation, the documents specified in section 215E of the Companies Act must be filed with the Registrar. Upon the receipt of the relevant documents and fees, the Registrar shall issue a notice of amalgamation. The effective date of the amalgamation is the date shown on such notice of amalgamation, which is either the date of filing with the Registrar or the date specified in the amalgamation proposal on which the amalgamation is intended to be effective (if it is to be on or after the date of such filing).

[78] On the effective date of the amalgamation, all property, rights and privileges of each amalgamating company are transferred to and vested in the amalgamated company. All liabilities and obligations of each amalgamating company are transferred to and become liabilities and obligations of the amalgamated company.

5.6 Shareholder Disclosures

[79] The Take-over Code provides that parties to a takeover transaction and their associates (as defined in the Take-over Code) are free to trade in the target company's shares but are subject to additional disclosure obligations during the offer period. The parties to a takeover and their associates are required to disclose shares, options or derivatives purchased or sold by them on their own account on a daily basis. The term 'associate' will normally include a holder of 5% or more of the equity share capital of the offeror or target company.

[80] Disclosure has to be made to the SGX-ST and the SIC. Dealings by an offeror or the target company or by an associate may be disclosed by the party concerned or by an agent, for instance, an investment bank or stockbroker, who acts on its behalf. Where there is more than one agent, particular care should be taken to ensure that the responsibility for disclosure is agreed between the parties and that it is neither overlooked nor duplicated.

[81] Apart from the Take-over Code, shareholder disclosure obligations are found in the SFA and are required by the SGX-ST with regard to listed companies. Disclosure obligations arise when a shareholder becomes a substantial shareholder, being a shareholder who has an 'interest' (as defined by the SFA) of 5% or more of the total votes attached to all the voting shares in a company. Disclosure must subsequently be made if there is a change in the substantial shareholder's 'percentage level' of interest in voting shares in a company. 'Percentage level' is defined in section 136(3) of the SFA. In summary, substantial shareholders are required to make disclosure of changes in their interest in threshold bands of 1%. Disclosure is required to be made by the shareholder to the listed company under the SFA. The listed company is required to, under the SFA, announce to the public the notification by the substantial shareholder through SGXNet.

5.7 Insider Dealing

[82] If an offeror is in possession of price-sensitive information regarding the target company, it cannot deal in the target company's shares until such information has become public or is no longer price-sensitive. In the context of a takeover, being in possession of price-sensitive information would prevent the offeror from making the bid unless the information is disclosed to all the shareholders of the target company as well.

[83] The provisions relating to insider dealing are found in the SFA. An insider dealer may be subject to criminal prosecution, a civil action taken by an aggrieved investor, as well as a civil action taken by the MAS.

5.8 Types of Takeover Offers

[84] Takeover offers may generally take three forms under the Take-over Code. An offer may be either a mandatory offer or a voluntary offer. It could also be a partial offer, in which the offeror does not seek to obtain 100% of the shares in the target company. An offeror can seek irrevocable undertakings from the shareholders of the target company to accept its offer. Such undertakings must be publicly disclosed.

[85] Where a company has more than one class of equity share capital, the Take-over Code provides that a comparable offer must be made for each class, and the SIC must be consulted in advance in such cases. The Take-over Code also provides that where a target company has convertible securities in issue, the offeror shall also make an appropriate offer to the holders of those convertible issues. The Notes to the Take-over Code provide guidance on the appropriate offer price for instruments convertible into, rights to subscribe for, and options in respect of, securities being offered or which carry voting rights.

5.9 Mandatory Offers

[86] Generally, there are no restrictions on an offeror building a significant stake in a target company as long as a mandatory offer is not triggered. The circumstances wherein mandatory offers are triggered are set out in the Take-over Code. Rule 14 of the Take-over Code provides that a mandatory offer is triggered when an offeror acquires, whether by a series of transactions over a period of time or not, shares which taken together with shares held or acquired by persons acting in concert with it amount to 30% or more of shares carrying voting rights of the target company. A mandatory offer is also triggered when an offeror and persons acting in concert with it hold between 30% and 50% of the target company's shares carrying voting rights and acquire in aggregate more than 1% of the target company's shares carrying voting rights in any rolling six-month period. For these purposes, a person who has acquired or written any option or derivative which causes him to have a long economic exposure to changes in the price of securities will normally be treated as having acquired those securities and persons who would breach the relevant thresholds by acquiring such derivatives must consult the SIC beforehand to determine if an offer is required and if so, the terms on which such offer is to be made.

[87] In a mandatory offer, the offer price cannot be lower than the highest price paid by the offeror or any of the parties acting in concert with it for any shares carrying voting rights during the offer period and during the six months leading up to the beginning of the offer period. The consideration paid in the mandatory offer must be in cash or be accompanied by a cash alternative. A mandatory offer is conditional upon the offeror obtaining acceptances which will result in the offeror and persons acting in concert with it holding shares carrying more than 50% of the voting rights of the target company. Generally, no other conditions are permitted to be imposed in a mandatory offer. An exception to this rule applies to a mandatory offer where the parties are seeking clearance with the Competition and Consumer Commission of Singapore (CCCS) under the Competition Act. In such a situation, the SIC will allow an additional condition relating to the CCCS process to be imposed; this is discussed under 'Competition Aspects' below.

Chain Principle

[88] Where an offeror acquires more than 50% of the voting shares of a target company and the target company holds 30% or more of the voting shares of a public company, which is subject to the Take-over Code, and as a result, the offeror acquires or consolidates control of the public company because the target company itself had effective control (i.e., 30% or more of the voting shares) of the public company, the offeror may be required to make a mandatory takeover offer for the public company. Note 7 to Rule 14.1 of the Take-over Code provides that the SIC will not normally require an offer to be made in these circumstances unless the Singapore public company constitutes or contributes significantly to the target company in respect of assets, market capitalization (where both companies are listed), sales or earnings. The SIC should be consulted in all cases which may come within the scope of Note 7 to Rule 14.1 to establish whether, in the circumstances, any obligation arises to make a mandatory offer.

Whitewash

[89] In certain situations, for example, one which involves a 'back door listing', the SIC may, on application, grant a waiver to an offeror from making a mandatory takeover offer. Such a waiver is typically subject to the condition that a majority of the independent shareholders present at a general meeting of the target company approve, on a poll, a separate resolution (typically referred to as a 'whitewash' resolution) waiving their rights to receive a takeover offer. The offeror and persons acting in concert with it must abstain from voting on the whitewash resolution.

[90] The Whitewash Guidance Note in Appendix 1 of the Take-over Code sets out the procedure to be followed if the SIC is to be asked to waive the obligation to make a mandatory offer under Rule 14 of the Take-over Code which would otherwise arise where, as a result of the issue of new securities as consideration for an acquisition, or a cash injection, or in fulfilment of obligations under an agreement to underwrite the issue of new securities, or whereupon the exercise of conversion of convertibles by a person or group of persons acting in concert, an obligation to make a general offer arises.

5.10 Voluntary Offers

[91] A voluntary offer is an offer made for all the shares of the target company which does not trigger the mandatory offer rules in Rule 14 of the Take-over Code. Voluntary offers are subject to Rule 15 of the Take-over Code. An offeror can make a voluntary offer at any time unless it becomes obliged to make a mandatory offer. A voluntary offer must always be conditional on the offeror and its concert parties acquiring more than 50% of the target company. In addition, the offeror can stipulate other objective conditions such as a particular level of acceptances, shareholders' approval and certain regulatory approvals. The SIC should be consulted where conditions are attached. In the case of voluntary offers conditional on a high level of acceptances, that is, a level which is higher than 50%, the SIC will allow such offers where the offeror states clearly in the offer document the level of acceptances upon which the offer is conditional and the offeror satisfies the SIC that it is acting in good faith in imposing such a high level of acceptance. Generally speaking, the conditions which may be attached to a voluntary offer must not be of a kind whose fulfilment is dependent on the subjective interpretation or discretion of the offeror. As an exception to this rule, the SIC allows an offeror to subject a voluntary (but not mandatory) offer to a condition that the CCCS issues a favourable decision allowing the voluntary offer to proceed on terms acceptable to the offeror.

[92] Note 4 to Rule 15.1 of the Take-over Code provides that the SIC will consider allowing the offeror to revise the initial acceptance level to a lower level (but above the 50% as required by Rule 15.1) during the course of the voluntary offer, provided the revised offer remains open for another fourteen days following the date written notification is despatched to shareholders of the revision. In addition, shareholders who have accepted the initial offer should be permitted to withdraw their acceptance within eight days of notification of the revision. The revised acceptance level will take into account withdrawals and new acceptances as at the close of the offer.

[93] In a voluntary offer, the offer price cannot be lower than the highest price paid by the offeror or any of its concert parties for any shares carrying voting rights in the target company during the offer period and within the three months leading up to the beginning of the offer period. The consideration offered may be in the form of cash or securities or a combination of both.

[94] The Take-over Code provides that where the offeror and/or any of its concert parties have bought for cash during the offer period, and within six months prior to its commencement, shares of the target company carrying 10% or more of the voting rights of that class, then an offer must be in cash or accompanied by a cash alternative at not less than the highest price paid by the offeror or any concert parties during the offer period and within six months prior to its commencement. A cash offer may also be required where, in the view of the SIC, there are circumstances which render such a course necessary.

[95] In addition, when the offeror and any of its concert parties purchase target company shares carrying 10% or more of voting rights in exchange for securities during the offer period and in the three months prior to the commencement of the offer period, such securities will normally be required to be offered to all other holders of shares of that class in a takeover offer.

[96] The SIC is given the discretion to require securities to be offered even in cases where the amount purchased is less than 10%, or the purchase took place more than three months prior to the commencement of the offer period, where the vendors are directors or otherwise closely connected with the offeror or the target company.

[97] The SIC should be consulted when 10% or more of the voting rights of the target company has been acquired during the offer period and in the six months prior to the commencement of the offer period for a mixture of securities and cash.

5.11 Partial Offers

[98] Partial offers are voluntary offers for less than 100% of the outstanding shares in a target company. The provisions relating to partial offers are found in Rule 16 of the Take-over Code. All partial offers must be approved by the SIC and Rule 16 sets out situations where the offeror makes an offer for less than 30%, for between 30% and 50%, and for between 50% and 100% of the target company's shares carrying voting rights.

[99] The Take-over Code provides that the SIC will normally grant consent for a partial offer which does not result in the offeror and persons acting in concert with its holding shares carrying 30% or more of the voting rights of the target company. There is no requirement for a target company to seek competent, independent advice for partial offers that result in an offeror holding less than 30%.

[100] The SIC will not grant consent in the case of a partial offer which could result in the offeror and its concert parties holding shares carrying not less than 30% but not more than 50% of the voting rights of the target company.

[101] In the case of a partial offer which could result in the offeror and its concert parties holding shares carrying more than 50% but less than 100% of the voting rights of the target company, consent will not normally be granted by the SIC unless the conditions set out in Rule 16.4 of the Take-over Code are satisfied. These conditions include the requirement that the partial offer is not a mandatory offer under Rule 14 of the Take-over Code and that the offeror and parties acting in concert with it must not acquire shares in the target company six months prior to the announcement and in the period between applying for approval from the SIC and making the partial offer and during the offer period and during the six-month period after the close of the partial offer.

[102] The Take-over Code also provides that the SIC will not normally consent to a partial offer which could result in the offeror and its concert parties holding more than 50% of the voting rights of the target company unless the partial offer is conditional, not only on the specified number or percentage of acceptances being received but also on approval by the target company's shareholders, where the offeror together with parties acting in concert with it hold 50% or less in the target company prior to the announcement of the partial offer. Where the offeror and its concert parties already hold more than 50% of the voting rights of the target company, approval of the target company's shareholders would be required if the partial offer could result in the offeror and its concert parties holding more than 90% of the target company, or the target company breaching the minimum free float requirement under the Listing Manual. The offeror, parties acting in concert with it, and their associates are not allowed to vote on the partial offer. In a Take-over Bulletin issued in January 2018, the SIC clarified that for a partial offer for more than 50% of the target company, the partial offer must be conditional on a precise number of shares or percentage, and that the SIC would not approve a partial offer where the Offeror and its concert parties could end up with a range of shareholding. In practice, this would mean that if an Offeror and its concert parties hold shares in the target, the partial offer should be made for a specified percentage of shares of the target company (excluding those held by the Offeror and its concert parties).

[103] Generally, the provisions in the Take-over Code applicable to a voluntary offer will also apply to partial offers and the documents required for a voluntary offer will also be required in a partial offer. Consideration for a partial offer may be in the form of cash or securities, or a combination of both. As with a voluntary offer, if the offeror and its concert parties had purchased for cash, shares carrying 10% or more of the voting rights of the target company during the offer period and in the six months prior to the commencement of a partial offer, the consideration offered must, in the case of a partial offer for less than 30%[2], be in cash or accompanied by a cash alternative at not less than the highest price paid for shares in the target company by the offeror and its concert parties during the offer period and in the six months prior to the commencement of the partial offer. Likewise, when the purchase was made in exchange for securities, such securities will normally be required to be offered to all other holders of shares of that class.

5.12 Private Acquisitions

[104] The acquisition of shares in private companies is largely unregulated, aside from merger controls, and parties are generally free to agree on the terms of the acquisition of shares or assets of the target company subject to a few statutory exceptions (e.g., section 18A of the Employment Act 1968) (*see* paragraph 211] below).

[105] It is customary for an acquirer to require due diligence to be conducted on the target company. However, there is no legal obligation imposed on the owner of a target company or the target to assist the acquirer with its enquiries or to make any disclosure. Hence, an acquirer seeks protection and comfort through thorough due diligence and providing extensive warranties and indemnities in the purchase agreement.

[106] The main objective of a due diligence exercise is, of course, to identify legal, financial or commercial obstacles and issues which challenge any basis or assumption of the acquirer in its offer, affect the valuation of the target or the unencumbered ability of the acquirer to own or deal with the assets or continue the business following the acquisition, or otherwise affect the successful closing of the deal.

[107] Where information and records are maintained in public registers, for example, the creation of certain debentures and charges by a Singapore company, title in real property and ownership of trademarks, etc., access to such information and records is easy and fast. Otherwise, the extent of disclosure and the availability of information would depend on the transparency of the owner and his readiness to disclose and this, at least in part, accounts for the importance of warranties and indemnities.

[108] The tension between an acquirer and the owner is usually focused on the scope of the warranties and indemnities and the limitations on the acquirer's right to claim under those provisions, for example, the period of the claim, the maximum liability of the owner, the minimum threshold before a claim can be made, etc.

[2] As highlighted above, one of the conditions for a partial offer for more than 50% is that the Offeror and its concert parties cannot acquire any shares in the six months preceding the announcement of the partial offer.

6 COMPETITION ASPECTS

6.1 Merger Control Generally

[109] In Singapore, the general merger control regime is prescribed under the Competition Act, which is the principal statute governing the competition law regime in Singapore. The statutory authority which oversees and administers the general competition law regime in Singapore is the CCCS, a statutory board of the Ministry of Trade and Industry, established under the Competition Act.

[110] Section 54 of the Competition Act prohibits mergers that have resulted or may be expected to result, in a substantial lessening of competition (SLC) within any market affecting Singapore for goods and services (the 'section 54 Prohibition'). The section 54 Prohibition may apply even where the merger takes place outside of Singapore, or where any merger is outside Singapore, so long as the merger has resulted, or may be expected to result, in an SLC within any market in Singapore.

[111] In addition to the Competition Act, the CCCS has also issued a set of guidelines which are officially gazetted documents, which indicate how the CCCS will interpret and give effect to the Competition Act. The CCCS guidelines provide a conceptual and analytical framework for the CCCS in its analysis and evaluation of cases and serve as a guide as to how the CCCS interprets and implements the competition law regime. It is important to note that the guidelines do not purport to represent a full or binding statement of law. For the purposes of merger control, the CCCS issued the *Guidelines on the Substantive Assessment of Mergers* and the *Guidelines on Merger Procedures*, both of which were published in June 2007. These guidelines have subsequently undergone a few revisions, with the latest versions being the revised *Guidelines on Merger Procedures* and the revised *Guidelines on the Substantive Assessment of Mergers*, both of which came into effect on 1 February 2022.

6.2 Notifiable Transactions

[112] Transactions which constitute a 'merger' under section 54 of the Competition Act are notifiable to the CCCS under its merger control regime. Under the Competition Act, a merger is deemed to occur when:

- two or more undertakings, previously independent from one another, merge;
- one or more persons or other undertakings acquire direct or indirect control of the whole or part of one or more other undertakings; or
- an acquisition by one undertaking (the first undertaking) of the assets (including goodwill), or a substantial part of the assets, of another undertaking (the second undertaking), places the first undertaking in a position to replace or substantially replace the second undertaking in the business or, as

appropriate, the part concerned of the business in which that undertaking was engaged immediately before the acquisition.

[113] The term 'undertaking' is defined under the Competition Act to mean any person, being an individual, a body corporate, an unincorporated body of persons or any other entity, capable of carrying on commercial or economic activities relating to goods or services. However, where all of the undertakings involved in the merger are, directly or indirectly, under the control of the same undertaking, the transaction will not constitute a merger under the Competition Act.

[114] 'Control' in relation to an undertaking exists if, by reason of rights, contracts or any other means, or any combination of rights, contracts or other means, decisive influence is capable of being exercised with regard to the activities of the undertaking and, in particular by:

- ownership of, or the right to use all or part of, the assets of an undertaking; or
- rights or contracts which enable decisive influence to be exercised with regard to the composition, voting or decisions of the organs of an undertaking.

[115] The CCCS generally considers that decisive influence is deemed to exist when the transaction results in ownership of more than 50% of the voting rights (attributable to the share capital of an undertaking which is currently exercisable at a general meeting). Where the transaction results in the ownership of between 30% and 50% of the voting rights, there is a rebuttable presumption that decisive influence exists. However, these thresholds are only indicative, and control could potentially be established at levels below these thresholds if other relevant factors provide strong evidence of control. Other forms of voting rights will also be taken into account in assessing control.

[116] Besides establishing legal ownership through the acquisition of rights and securities, de facto control may also be established. As there is no precise criterion for determining when an acquirer gains de facto control of an undertaking's activities, the CCCS will adopt a case-by-case approach to taking into account all relevant circumstances.

[117] Control can, therefore, exist where minority shareholders are conferred decisive influence with regard to the activities of an undertaking. This can be established on a legal and/or de facto basis. Legally, it can occur where minority shareholders have additional rights that allow them to veto decisions that are essential for the strategic commercial behaviour of the undertaking, such as the budget, business plans, major investments, the appointment of senior management or market-specific rights. A minority shareholder can also be deemed to have sole control on a de facto basis where it is highly likely to achieve control over decisions made at any shareholders' meeting, due to patterns of attendance and voting at these meetings and the fact that the remaining shares are widely dispersed.

[118] The Competition Act also provides that the creation of a joint venture, which is broadly defined under the *Guidelines on the Substantive Assessment of Mergers* as a collaborative arrangement by which two or more undertakings devote their resources to pursue a common objective, may also fall within the definition of a 'merger' under the Competition Act, if the joint venture is one that is subject to joint control and performs, on a lasting basis, all the functions of an autonomous economic entity.

6.3 Mergers Outside Singapore

[119] As outlined above, the section 54 Prohibition is applicable to merger situations which take place both in Singapore and other countries, so long as the merger could impact competition in markets affecting Singapore. Accordingly, it is not possible to exclude the need for a filing even where the target is not present in Singapore (i.e., has no local turnover, no local assets and no corporate entity present in the jurisdiction).

As a case in point, the CCCS issued a provisional statement of decision (on 25 May 2018) on the proposed acquisition by Wilhelmsen Maritime Services AS (WMS) of Drew Marine Group Coöperatief U.A. and Drew Marine Partners L.P.'s technical solutions, fire, safety and rescue businesses in the marine chemicals sector in Singapore. The parties were both foreign-incorporated companies, but the CCCS was prepared to block the acquisition because it potentially resulted in an SLC in Singapore.

6.4 Anti-competitive Mergers

[120] As set out above, a merger is prohibited by the Competition Act where it has resulted or may be expected to result, in an SLC within any market in Singapore for goods or services, subject to any exclusions, exemptions or net economic efficiencies applicable under the Competition Act. In determining whether an SLC exists, the CCCS will evaluate the prospects for competition in the future, by comparing the likely state of competition if the merger situation proceeds, with the likely state of competition if the merger situation does not proceed.

[121] As a starting point, the level of concentration in a market can be an indicator of competitive pressure. In examining market concentration and structure, the CCCS focuses on market shares and concentration ratios. While there are no jurisdictional safe harbours where mergers which do not trigger specified quantitative thresholds are exempt or excluded from the section 54 Prohibition, the CCCS is generally likely to give further consideration to a merger if it meets the following indicative notification thresholds:

- the merged undertaking will have a market share of 40% or more; or
- the merged undertaking will have a market share of between 20% and 40% and the post-merger combined market share of the three largest firms is 70% or more, (the 'Quantitative Thresholds').

The Quantitative Thresholds are calculated based on the 'relevant market', which is identified generally by the application of the hypothetical monopolist test.

The definition of the relevant market involves defining the product market and the geographic market. The relevant product market is determined by considering which products would be regarded as substitutes for the focal product on the demand side and the supply side. The geographic market can usually be defined as local (Singapore), regional or global.

[122] The *Guidelines on Merger Procedures* have also introduced an indicative turnover threshold in that the CCCS is unlikely to investigate a merger situation that only involves small companies, namely where:

- the turnover in Singapore in the financial year preceding the transaction of each of the parties is below SGD5 m (approx. USD3.62 m); and
- the combined worldwide turnover in the financial year preceding the transaction of all the parties is below SGD50 m (approx. USD36.2 m), (the '*De Minimis* Thresholds').

[123] The CCCS generally expects that notifications are made where the Quantitative Thresholds are crossed within the broader identified markets or narrower market segments. Notwithstanding this, the thresholds set out in paragraph [121] are simply indicators of potential competition concerns but do not give rise to a presumption on whether the merger situation will lessen competition substantially. In this regard, a significant number of mergers reviewed and investigated by the CCCS had involved concentrations which fall below the Quantitative Thresholds, as an SLC could potentially be established below such thresholds, if other relevant factors, such as the following, provide strong evidence of any SLC:

- actual and potential competition in the market;
- barriers to entry; and
- countervailing buyer power.

Hence, merger situations should be notified to the CCCS if there is a risk that the merger may result in an SLC in any market affecting Singapore, notwithstanding that the Quantitative Thresholds are not crossed.

6.5 Exclusions and Exemptions under the Competition Act

[124] The Competition Act allows the CCCS to take efficiency gains into account at two separate points in the analytical framework:

- first, efficiencies may be taken into account where they increase rivalry in the market so that no SLC would result from a merger; and
- second, efficiencies may be taken into account where they do not avert an SLC but will nevertheless result in net economic efficiencies in markets in Singapore. Such efficiencies should bring about lower costs, greater innovation, greater choice or quality and be sufficient to outweigh the detriments to competition in Singapore caused by the merger. Consequently, mergers with

net economic efficiencies are deemed to be excluded from the ambit of Singapore's merger control regime.

[125] Further, the section 54 Prohibition does not apply to any merger specified in the Fourth Schedule of the Competition Act, namely where the merger is:

- approved by any Minister or regulatory authority (other than the CCCS) pursuant to any requirement for such approval imposed by any written law;
- approved by the MAS pursuant to any requirement for such approval imposed under any written law; or
- under the jurisdiction of another regulatory authority (other than the CCCS), under any written law or code of practice relating to competition.

[126] The section 54 Prohibition also does not apply to any merger involving an undertaking in relation to certain specified activities, which are defined in paragraph 6(2) of the Third Schedule of the Competition Act. The specified activities tend to relate to the supply of services for the public, which are:

- the supply of ordinary letter and postcard services by a person licensed and regulated under the Postal Services Act 1999;
- the supply of piped potable water;
- the supply of wastewater management services;
- the supply of bus services by licensed bus operators under the Bus Services Industry Act 2015;
- the supply of rail services by any person licensed and regulated under the Rapid Transit Systems Act 1995; and
- cargo terminal operators carried out by a person licensed and regulated under the Maritime and Port of Authority of Singapore Act 1996.

6.6 Mandatory Self-assessment

[127] The Singapore merger control regime is a risk-based, voluntary one. If merger parties require deal certainty and do not want the merger to carry any anti-trust risk, they may nevertheless notify their merger situations to the CCCS and apply for a decision as to whether the merger has infringed or the anticipated merger, if carried into effect, will infringe the section 54 Prohibition (an application). Filing fees must be paid to the CCCS when making a merger notification.

[128] A decision on whether or not to file an application must, therefore, be made on the basis of a mandatory self-assessment conducted in accordance with the guidelines published by the CCCS and read with its decided cases. The self-assessment is to be documented in the form of an email, dated memorandum or note which the CCCS would accept as documentary evidence of a mandatory Singapore merger control self-assessment having been conducted contemporaneously with the transaction. This should be retained on file by the merging parties and may be provided to the CCCS as a first line of defence in the event that the CCCS asks to review the transaction, in particular, to argue that any infringement was not entered into intentionally or negligently (*see* the section below on 'Consequences of

Infringing the Section 54 Prohibition'). Following self-assessment, where the decision is taken to make an application, the merger parties should include such an obligation as a condition precedent.

[129] Failure to notify a notifiable merger to the CCCS before consummation of the merger may be construed by the CCCS as 'intentionally or negligently' infringing the section 54 Prohibition.

As a case in point, it should be noted that the CCCS cited the failure to notify a merger which has or is expected to result in an SLC prior to the commencement of the CCCS's investigation of the merger as an intentional or negligent infringement of the section 54 Prohibition in its infringement decision for the acquisition of Uber Technologies, Inc.'s ('Uber') South East Asian business by Grab Inc. ('Grab') and Uber's acquisition of a 27.5% stake in Grab ('Grab/Uber').

[130] If the CCCS subsequently decides (acting on its own or on a third-party complaint) that the merger in question results or would result in an SLC, the CCCS may impose structural or behavioural remedies on the merger parties, such as a direction for the merger to be unwound or for divestments to be carried out. Where infringement has been committed 'intentionally or negligently', the CCCS may impose financial penalties of up to 10% of the parties' turnover in Singapore for each year of infringement for such period as may be prescribed, up to a maximum of three years.

6.7 Risks of Not Filing

[131] In the absence of a filing, merger parties bear an evergreen risk that the CCCS can investigate a merger or an anticipated merger on its own initiative (under section 62 of the Competition Act) and has the power to unwind a merger that has already been effected and, in the case of intentional or negligent infringements, to impose financial penalties if it decides that the merger infringes the section 54 Prohibition (*see* the section below on 'Consequences of Infringing the Section 54 Prohibition').

[132] While Singapore's merger control regime is non-suspensory, the CCCS can impose interim measures to prevent any action that may prejudice the CCCS's ability to investigate the merger situation or its ability to impose appropriate remedies:

- On 13 April 2018, the CCCS issued its first-ever Notice of Interim Measures Directions (IMD) in *Grab/Uber*. The interim directions imposed on Grab include, among others, the maintenance of pre-transaction pricing, product options, and commission rates, holding separate of certain operational data, the removal of exclusivity obligations for new drivers and the appointment of a Monitoring Trustee.
- On 24 September 2018, the CCCS issued an Infringement Decision for *Grab/Uber*. The CCCS concluded that the acquisition has substantially lessened competition and imposed directions and fines of SGD13 m (approx. USD9.46 m) on the parties. It is noteworthy that the CCCS commenced its

investigation, notwithstanding the parties' announced intention to voluntarily lodge a post-completion merger notification to the CCCS, which the Singapore merger control regime allows for.

[133] In the absence of a filing, merger parties also bear the risk that a CCCS investigation, which may be triggered at any point pre or post-closing of the transaction, may adversely affect the timeline for the closing of the transaction or for implementation of the transaction post-closing. There is no administrative timetable for an investigation, and the investigation can take several months to several years. Further, when the CCCS investigates, the CCCS is likely to have formed its own theories of harm, and the practical burden of proof, which will be on the merger parties, would be significantly harder to discharge.

[134] The CCCS continues to actively investigate mergers that have not been notified, which are triggered through the CCCS's market intelligence functions or by third-party complaints. As a case in point, the CCCS, on 23 March 2018, initiated an investigation into a merger that has been completed for more than five years under section 62 of the Competition Act. The CCCS has also previously raised serious doubts as to the compatibility of transactions with section 54 of the Competition Act, even where:

- mergers by the same parties, or involving the same industry, had received clearances in other jurisdictions;
- there are no significant issues identified within thc wider defined relevant markets, but the CCCS has reviewed whether there may be competition issues within narrower market segments, on a global or Singapore-specific basis; or
- the indicative quantitative thresholds are not crossed.

6.8 Filing a Merger Notification to the CCCS

[135] The CCCS adopts a two-phased approach when evaluating notified anticipated mergers and mergers:

- Phase 1 Review: The CCCS commences a Phase 1 Review after it accepts a completed Form M1 which fulfils all the applicable filing requirements, including the receipt of the relevant filing fee. The indicative administrative timeframe for a Phase 1 Review is thirty working days. Anticipated mergers and mergers that clearly do not raise any competition concerns will be cleared under the Phase 1 Review.
- Phase 2 Review: If the CCCS is unable, based on the information submitted during the Phase 1 Review, to conclude that the anticipated merger or merger does not raise any competition concerns, it will proceed to a Phase 2 Review. A Phase 2 Review entails a more detailed assessment and is expected to be completed within 120 working days from when the CCCS receives a complete Form M2 and a response to the Phase 2 information request that

the CCCS deems satisfactory. To date, approximately one out of five mergers notified to the CCCS has proceeded to a Phase 2 Review.

[136] The merger review time frames are not binding on the CCCS, although the CCCS will endeavour to keep within the said time frames. Notably, during the Phase 1 and Phase 2 Review periods, the CCCS may require the applicant to provide additional information within a certain deadline. If the applicant is unable to respond with the additional information within the deadline, the CCCS may 'stop the clock' for the period between the deadline and the subsequent point where the applicant responds with the additional information. If the applicant fails to respond with the additional information within the deadline (and any extensions which may have been granted), the CCCS may determine the application by not giving a decision, but may then commence its own investigation into the merger using its statutory powers.

[137] Further, the CCCS may, at any time before making a decision as to whether the section 54 Prohibition has been or will be infringed, accept commitments from the merger parties that remedy, mitigate or prevent the SLC arising from the merger. This may also result in an extension of the applicable deadline where the CCCS 'stops the clock' to consider such commitments.

[138] Upon commencement of the Phase 1 Review, the CCCS will publish the details of an accepted application on its public register and invite interested third parties to provide their comments on the merger. The entry will be updated if CCCS is considering whether or not to accept commitments if the merger proceeds to a Phase 2 Review and once the CCCS takes a decision under section 54 of the Competition Act. Third parties are invited to comment on the merger via an invitation to comment on the CCCS website and when the CCCS consults on commitments. The CCCS may also approach third parties such as customers, suppliers and competitors directly for information.

[139] Where the CCCS has issued a decision that a merger has not infringed or that an anticipated merger will not, if carried into effect, infringe the section 54 Prohibition, immunity is conferred in that the CCCS will not take further action in relation to the section 54 Prohibition, unless:

- the CCCS has reasonable grounds for suspecting that the information on which it based its decision (including any information on the basis for which it accepted a commitment) was incomplete, false or misleading; or
- the CCCS has reasonable grounds for suspecting that a party who provided a commitment failed to adhere to one or more of the commitment terms.

Further, a decision that an anticipated merger will not, if carried into effect infringes the section 54 Prohibition may also be subject to a validity period, in which such immunity will apply only where the anticipated merger is carried into effect within the validity period. In the CCCS's recent decisions, the validity period is typically one year.

[140] In addition, agreements, arrangements or provisions which are directly related and necessary to the implementation of the merger may also benefit from the CCCS's decision that a merger has not infringed or an anticipated merger will not, if carried into effect, infringe the section 54 Prohibition by an exemption from prohibitions against anti-competitive agreements and abuse of dominance in the Competition Act.

[141] Where the CCCS proposes to issue a decision that a merger has infringed or an anticipated merger will, if carried into effect, infringe the section 54 Prohibition, it will give notice to the party who applied for the decision, or where that party no longer exists, the merged entity. The CCCS will also give the applicant an opportunity to make written representations to the CCCS and to inspect the documents in the CCCS file. Further, that party may, within fourteen days of the notice, apply to the Minister for Trade and Industry for the anticipated merger or merger to be exempted from the section 54 Prohibition on the ground of any public interest consideration. To date, the CCCS has issued three provisional statements of decision proposing to prohibit notified mergers in April 2010, March 2015 and May 2018, although the CCCS subsequently cleared the earlier merger after considering written submissions filed by the parties. There were also four other merger notifications lodged with the CCCS which were subsequently withdrawn by the merger parties which may have been due to serious concerns expressed by the CCCS.

[142] There is also a right of appeal to the Competition Appeal Board against any final decision by the CCCS in respect of a merger situation or any direction (including interim measures imposed by the CCCS). Any merger party may make an appeal against the CCCS's final decision in respect of a merger situation, while an appeal against a direction may be made by the person to whom the CCCS gave the direction. An appeal must be brought within the time period specified in the Competition (Appeals) Regulations.

6.9 Consequences of Infringing the Section 54 Prohibition

[143] In the event of a CCCS finding that a merger or an anticipated merger gives rise to an infringement of the section 54 Prohibition, the CCCS may impose structural or behavioural remedies on the merger parties, such as a direction for the merger to be unwound or for divestments to be carried out.

[144] The CCCS will also consider whether the infringement was intentionally or negligently committed in determining whether financial penalties should be levied on the merger parties. The CCCS may impose financial penalties of up to 10% of the parties' turnover in Singapore for each year of infringement for such period as may be prescribed, up to a maximum of three years.

[145] Further, parties suffering loss or damage directly arising from a merger that has infringed the section 54 Prohibition are entitled to commence a civil action seeking relief against the relevant undertakings. Such rights of private action only arise after the CCCS has made a decision that a merger has infringed the section

54 Prohibition and the appeal period has expired or, where an appeal has been brought, upon determination of the appeal.

6.10 Confidential Advice

[146] To assist with planning and consideration of future mergers, in particular at the stage when the merger parties are concerned to preserving the confidentiality of the transaction, the CCCS is prepared to give confidential advice on whether or not a merger is likely to raise competition concerns in Singapore and therefore whether a notification is advisable, with the necessary qualification that such advice is provided without having taken into account third-party views. The CCCS expects to provide confidential advice within fourteen working days of receipt of all the required information.

[147] Confidential advice is only available if the CCCS is satisfied that the following conditions are met:

- that all parties to the anticipated merger intend to carry into effect the anticipated merger;
- that no information relating to the anticipated merger is in the public domain at the time that the application for confidential advice is made; and
- if information relating to the anticipated merger enters the public domain after the application for confidential advice is made, that there are good reasons for the applicant not notifying the CCCS of the anticipated merger and not applying to the CCCS for a decision on whether the anticipated merger would result in an SLC under section 57 of the Competition Act.

This is so that the CCCS can manage its resources appropriately. In particular, confidential advice is available only for potential transactions which raise genuine issues relating to the competitive assessment in Singapore, where there is a good faith intention to proceed with the transactions, and which are not in the public domain.

[148] However, confidential advice does not amount to a decision under section 57 or 58 of the Competition Act. As such, confidential advice is not binding on the CCCS, and in all cases where confidential advice is given, the CCCS still reserves the right to investigate the merger situation.

6.11 Pre-notification Discussion

[149] The CCCS also gives merger parties the opportunity to request a Pre-Notification Discussion (PND). PNDs allow merger parties the opportunity to carry out informal discussions with the CCCS in order to identify the information to be submitted with the notification.

[150] PNDs permit the merger parties to ascertain what information the CCCS is likely to require in order for the CCCS's assessment of their transaction. During

PNDs, the CCCS does not give views on whether a merger situation would be likely to require a Phase 2 assessment, or if it would lead to an SLC.

[151] At the point when merger parties approach the CCCS for PNDs, merger parties should be in a position to show that there is a good faith intention to proceed with the transaction. It is possible to approach the CCCS for PNDs before there is a signed agreement.

[152] The CCCS does not stipulate a specific timeframe for the completion of the PND process. PNDs can be informal and brief, or more formal and prolonged, depending on the preference of the merger parties, the complexity of the transaction and the concerns that the merger may raise.

6.12 Recent Developments

[153] In 2018, the CCCS investigated the *Grab/Uber* transaction. The CCCS disagreed with the parties' definition of the relevant market and found the failure to notify the transaction prior to the commencement of the CCCS's investigation and the implementation of the transaction, among other things, to be an intentional and negligent infringement of Singapore competition laws, and imposed financial penalties of around SGD13 m, in addition to other directions. This has led to market observations that the CCCS merger regime is 'not truly voluntary'. The *Grab/Uber* investigation has also demonstrated that:

- the CCCS can reject a post-completion notification even though the Singapore merger control regime allows it, and conduct an investigation instead;
- the CCCS can refuse to accept commitments offered by parties, but elect to impose them as directions instead;
- the CCCS can impose financial penalties in a voluntary regime as a percentage of turnover (not capped at an absolute dollar figure), as it considers that the failure to make a pre-completion notification is a basis that the infringement is intentional or negligent; and
- if the CCCS disagrees with the parties' self-assessment (e.g., market definition), even though the parties did duly conduct a self-assessment, the CCCS can find that there was an intentional or negligent infringement by the parties in entering into the transaction.

[154] In 2018, the CCCS also called-in an unnotified transaction six years after the transaction had closed. This demonstrated the CCCS's willingness to call in transactions even though significant time had elapsed. It also reinforces the fact that there is no statute of limitation in Singapore on the CCCS's ability to review a transaction, and the antitrust risk for an unnotified transaction in Singapore is evergreen.

[155] On 25 May 2018, the CCCS issued a provisional statement of decision to block a foreign-to-foreign merger on the proposed acquisition by WMS of Drew

Marine Group Coöperatief U.A. and Drew Marine Partners L.P.'s technical solutions, fire, safety and rescue businesses in the marine chemicals sector in Singapore. Both parties were foreign-incorporated companies, but the CCCS was prepared to block the acquisition on the basis that it potentially results in an SLC in Singapore, and prior to other jurisdictions having made their decisions.

[156] The CCCS has also increasingly referred to commitments in its recent merger decisions with an emphasis on Singapore-specific effects. The notable examples are:

- on 13 November 2014, the CCCS issued its first conditional clearance requiring local behavioural and structural commitments in the proposed acquisition by SEEK Asia Investments Pte. Ltd. of 100% of the online recruitment business assets of JobStreet Corporation Berhad, including JobStreet.com Pte. Ltd. ('*SEEK/JobStreet*'). This also marked the first-ever market testing by the CCCS of proposed commitments offered by merger parties;
- on 11 March 2015, the CCCS issued letters to Fortis Healthcare Singapore Pte. Limited ('Fortis') and Parkway Holdings Ltd ('Parkway') on the provisional decision by the CCCS to block the proposed acquisition by Parkway, through its wholly owned subsidiary, Medi-Rad Associates Ltd, of RadLink-Asia Pte Limited and its subsidiaries from Fortis ('*RadLink/Parkway*'). The CCCS's decision to block RadLink/Parkway in 2015 followed less than five months after the CCCS's conditional clearance decision for *SEEK/JobStreet*. The CCCS was cited in media reports on its provisional decision on *RadLink/Parkway* articulating that no commitments were proposed to the CCCS for consideration during the review process;
- on 25 May 2018, the CCCS issued a provisional statement of decision on the proposed acquisition by WMS of Drew Marine Group Coöperatief U.A. and Drew Marine Partners L.P.'s technical solutions, fire, safety and rescue businesses in the marine chemicals sector in Singapore, and noted in its media release that the parties may offer commitments to address the potential competition concerns at any time before the CCCS issues its decision at the end of the Phase 2 Review; and
- on 24 May 2021, the CCCS conditionally cleared the proposed acquisition of Refinitiv Holdings Limited by London Stock Exchange Group plc. Although the merger parties had submitted commitments to other competition authorities overseas, the CCCS did not find those commitments sufficient to address its concerns relating to Singapore, and instead requested Singapore-specific commitments.

6.13 Likely Trends

[157] According to the Chief Executive of CCCS, Ms Sia Aik Kor, the CCCS will be focusing on the following areas in its administration and enforcement of the Competition Act:

- strengthening cooperation with regional competition authorities: strong regional cooperation will be a priority for the CCCS, in particular, to enable the CCCS to discuss complex issues with its counterparts in the region and to promote cooperation on competition cases between regulators. Examples of efforts toward greater regional cooperation include a handbook on e-commerce published by the CCCS in 2017, and the launch of the ASEAN Experts Group on Competition, or AEGC, an enforcers' network to link case handlers across the ASEAN countries in 2018. The increased cooperation and interactions between regional competition authorities would be a relevant factor to be considered when assessing the need for merger notifications in the region;
- focusing on e-commerce platforms: while the CCCS's market study on e-commerce platforms (published in September 2020) did not find any major competition concerns, the CCCS indicated that this would remain as an area of focus for the CCCS. This means that players active in the e-commerce space – especially operators of super apps (e-commerce platforms that integrate a range of distinct products and services in one app) – should continue to be vigilant and ensure that they are operating in a manner which is compliant with the Competition Act; and
- monitoring unnotified mergers: the CCCS conducts regular market surveillance to identify potentially anti-competitive mergers, and the CCCS will proactively investigate merger transactions – including killer acquisitions – that have not been notified, if it finds that there are reasonable grounds to suspect an infringement of the section 54 Prohibition has occurred or is likely to occur. In particular, the CCCS is closely monitoring mergers between e-commerce platforms that are active in different market segments.

[158] In terms of its case precedents, there is also an increasing trend of the CCCS looking into e-commerce and disruptive technologies, and studying their implications on competition policy in Singapore:

- One of the e-commerce-related mergers that the CCCS has looked at is *SEEK/JobStreet*. The transaction is ground-breaking in that it is the first merger review where the CCCS had considered two-sided platform markets, network effects, and the emerging divide between print media and online media in a dynamic market. The clearance is the first conditional clearance subject to local commitments offered in Singapore. Mergers cleared in Singapore by the CCCS previously pursuant to commitments had been on the basis of global commitments offered by merger parties in other jurisdictions.
- Most recently, the CCCS has set its sights on disruptive technologies in another two-sided market in the chauffeured personal point-to-point transport passenger and/or booking services market, specifically in relation to *Grab/Uber*, which is also a sector of keen consumer concern. In a seminal move on 13 April 2018, the CCCS issued IMD to the merging parties, in an attempt to ensure the market remains open and contestable, and for the purposes of preserving the pre-merger status-quo, up until the CCCS had fully reviewed the merger or if there were material changes to the conditions of the market that rendered the IMD otiose. The high-profile status of *Grab/*

Uber was underpinned by the substantial public interest in the matter and a large number of stakeholders. Multiple agencies and governmental regulators, such as the Land Transport Authority and the Ministry of Transport also took a keen interest, further adding to the furore of public interest. All in all, the CCCS has had to engage in multi-agency consultation and cooperation in what appears to be a historical and seminal case in Singapore.

[159] The CCCS has amplified its enforcement activity on merger control and is likely to:

- initiate an increased incidence of Phase 2 Reviews;
- increase merger probes in relation to unnotified mergers (particularly in the e-commerce sector) where there are likely to be effects on any markets affecting Singapore, as the CCCS has demonstrated increasingly aggressive enforcement towards merger control in Singapore through its horizon-scanning mechanisms to detect unnotified mergers proactively, and the formation of a Commitments and Remedies Unit (the CRU) to consider commitments and remedies required; and
- increasing focus on commitments for merger remedies with an emphasis on Singapore-specific effects and countervailing commitments. In this regard, the CCCS is likely to encourage commitment negotiations at the end of Phase 1 Reviews, early discussions with the CRU, market testing of proposed commitments and require upfront named buyers for divestiture commitments.

7 TAXATION ASPECTS

7.1 Taxation Issues on Acquisitions Generally

[160] Tax issues may arise in relation to the sale and purchase of business assets or shares in a company. Under the Income Tax Act 1947 (the 'Income Tax Act'), any income accruing in or derived from Singapore (sourced in Singapore) or accruing or derived from outside Singapore (sourced outside Singapore) and received in Singapore is subject to income tax in Singapore.

[161] Insofar as tax on gains is concerned, there is no imposition of capital gains tax in Singapore. Therefore, when the shareholders of a target company dispose of their target shares, the question is whether the gains, if any, constitute capital gains or trading income, the latter of which is subject to Singapore income tax. Whether the gains are treated as capital gains or trading income depends on whether the relevant shareholders of the target company are regarded by the Inland Revenue Authority of Singapore (IRAS) to be trading in shares or acquiring the shares with the intention of disposal for profit. If so, the next question that arises would be whether the gains are sourced in Singapore or sourced outside Singapore and received in Singapore. Certain 'safe harbour' rules have been enacted in Singapore whereby gains derived by a divesting company from its disposal of ordinary shares in an investee company during the period from 1 June 2012 to 31 December 2027 (both dates inclusive) are not taxable if certain conditions relating to particular shareholding thresholds and holding periods are met, and subject to certain exclusions. From 1 June 2022, such rules will also not apply to the disposal of unlisted shares in an investee company in the business of trading, holding or developing immovable properties in Singapore or outside Singapore. It is also possible to seek an advance ruling from the IRAS in respect of whether such gains would be treated as taxable in Singapore.

[162] Generally, the Income Tax Act permits a taxpayer to deduct the amount of loss incurred in any trade, business, profession or vocation, in determining its total statutory income chargeable with tax. In other words, a loss incurred in a trade, business, profession or vocation may reduce taxable income from other sources. In addition, allowances may be available in respect of capital expenditure incurred in the acquisition of certain assets for the purposes of a trade, profession or business (e.g., plant and machinery, intellectual property (IP) rights). In contrast, no allowances are available for capital expenditure incurred to produce passive income. Certain qualifying donations made by a taxpayer may also be claimed as deductions against taxable income.

[163] Subject to the respective conditions of each deduction scheme being met, any qualifying unabsorbed losses (which include trade losses, capital allowances and donations) may potentially be carried forward or backwards to reduce taxable income in another year of assessment, or may even be transferred to a group company.

[164] Where a share sale is involved, there may be issues of whether qualifying unabsorbed tax losses of the target company would remain available to the target company after the share sale if there was a substantial change in shareholders (as defined in the Income Tax Act) arising from the share sale.

[165] In contrast, where a business sale is involved, there may be issues of clawback of capital allowances (or tax depreciation) which have been claimed by the vendor as tax deductions in relation to the assets being sold. If the business sale involves the sale of inventory or stock-in-trade, there may also be issues relating to a deemed trading gain being imputed on the vendor.

[166] The tax treatment of tax resident ('Resident') and non-tax resident ('Non-Resident') vehicles does not differ materially under the Income Tax Act. However, Non-Residents cannot claim treaty benefits under Avoidance of Double Taxation Agreements or 'DTAs' signed between Singapore and other jurisdictions, of which Singapore has a wide network. Tax residence does not necessarily follow the jurisdiction of incorporation of the vehicle. Under domestic law, residence is generally dependent on whether the control and management of the business of the vehicle is exercised in Singapore (subject to specific provisions in applicable DTAs).

[167] Therefore, an offshore vehicle could possibly be regarded as a Resident, and an onshore vehicle could possibly be regarded as a Non-Resident depending on where the 'control and management' of its business is exercised. Some of the factors that might assist in establishing the Singapore tax residency of a company are as follows:

(1) the majority of the directors are Singapore residents;
(2) all directors' meetings are held in Singapore;
(3) the corporate documents of the company are kept in Singapore;
(4) the directors each act in an independent manner, that is, they exercise their functions as directors in a bona fide manner, and they do not act at the dictation of, or acquiesce to the decisions of, or suggestions made by, any other person or entity outside Singapore without proper consideration of their own;
(5) all tasks in relation to the running of the company and the execution of its business are the responsibility of the directors. The directors only delegate tasks for which they are responsible to:
   - employees, if any, of the company that are resident in Singapore;
   - professional service providers in Singapore under independent service contracts.
(6) no person outside Singapore has the general authority to negotiate and conclude any contracts on behalf of the company except in specific contractually delegated circumstances; and
(7) the company is incorporated in Singapore.

[168] The list of factors above is, of course, non-exhaustive and merely indicative. The determination of tax residency remains a question of fact (and can be quite formulistic in nature).

[169] The current corporate tax rate of 17% applies to both Resident and Non-Resident vehicles, and both Resident and Non-Resident vehicles should submit an income tax return to the IRAS on income taxable in Singapore. In the Singapore Budget Statement 2022, the Singapore government announced that in response to the minimum effective tax rate under the Organization for Economic Cooperation and Development (OECD) Pillar 2 Anti-Base Erosion rules of the BEPS 2.0 project, the Singapore government is exploring a top-up tax to top up a multinational enterprise (an MNE) group's effective tax rate in Singapore to 15% and such tax will apply to MNE groups operating in Singapore that have annual revenue of at least €750 m, as reflected in the consolidated financial statements of the ultimate parent entity. Singapore currently does not have a controlled foreign company regime, nor thin capitalization rules in place.

[170] All companies can enjoy partial tax exemption on their assessable income, in that 75% of the first SGD10 000 of income is tax-exempt, and 50% of the next SGD190 000 is tax-exempt. New 'start-up' companies will, subject to certain conditions, be eligible for tax exemption on three-quarters of their normal chargeable income of up to SGD100 000 and 50% of up to the next SGD100 000 of chargeable income a year for each of the company's first three years of assessment.

[171] In terms of transfer pricing considerations, the IRAS generally endorses the OECD's standards and is of the view that the arm's length principle is the most appropriate standard to determine transfer pricing for related-party transactions. The Income Tax Act also provides that where two persons are 'related parties' and conditions are made or imposed between the two persons in their commercial or financial relations which differ from those which would be made if they were not related parties, then any profits which would (but for those conditions) have accrued to one of the persons, and, by reason of those conditions, have not so accrued, may be included in the profits of that person and taxed in accordance with the provisions of the Income Tax Act. The term 'related party' in this context generally refers to situations where one entity directly or indirectly controls another, or where both entities concerned are under the control of a common person. Accordingly, the IRAS requires that an arm's length rate of interest be charged where related-party cross-border loans are concerned.

7.2 Stamp Duties

[172] Stamp duty in Singapore may be relevant to business and share acquisitions. In Singapore, stamp duty is generally levied on documents relating to the transfer or assignment of any interest in stocks, shares or immovable property. Stamp duty is payable within fourteen days from the date of execution if the document is executed in Singapore or thirty days of its receipt in Singapore if the document is executed overseas.

With respect to stamp duty on transfers of shares not subject to additional conveyance duties, stamp duty is generally payable on the transfer instrument transferring title over such shares (i.e., the transfer form).

In addition, the acquisition and disposal of certain equity interests in property holding entities that have a significant interest (directly or indirectly through other entities) in Singapore residential properties would also be subject to stamp duty as if such acquisition or disposal were a conveyance of the underlying interest in the residential properties.

Relief from stamp duty may be available under the Stamp Duties Act 1929 for transfers pursuant to the reconstruction or amalgamation of companies or transfers between 'associated permitted entities', provided that the conditions stipulated in the relevant subsidiary legislation are met. In this regard, the relevant subsidiary legislation are the Stamp Duties (Relief from Stamp Duty upon Reconstruction or Amalgamation of Companies) Rules (the 'Reconstruction or Amalgamation Rules') and the Stamp Duties (Relief from Stamp Duty upon Transfer of Assets between Associated Permitted Entities) Rules 2014 (the 'Transfer of Assets Rules').

[173] Certain broad conditions must be met in order to qualify for stamp duty relief under the Reconstruction or Amalgamation Rules, and the Transfer of Assets Rules. One main condition in relation to relief for the transfer of assets pursuant to a reconstruction or amalgamation of companies is that generally, the transferee company (i.e., the acquiring company) must increase its share capital with a view to acquiring no less than 90% of the 'reckonable' share capital (as defined in the Reconstruction or Amalgamation Rules), or the undertaking of the target company and that at least 90% of the consideration for the acquisition is satisfied by the issue of shares in the transferee company to the target company or the target company's shareholders. One main condition in relation to relief for the transfer of assets between 'associated permitted entities' is that the transferor and transferee entities must have been 'associated' with each other (within the meaning of the Transfer of Assets Rules) for at least twelve months prior to the transfer unless the transferee entity had been incorporated, specially to acquire the relevant assets.

[174] The availability of stamp duty relief under the Reconstruction or Amalgamation Rules, and the Transfer of Assets Rules, hinges on a formal application being made to the Commissioner of Stamp Duties, for the grant of such relief. If stamp duty relief is granted, it should be noted that such relief is generally subject to certain continuing obligations, the breach of which would result in the subsequent clawback of any stamp duty relief previously granted, and the imposition of interest at the rate of 6% per annum from the date on which duty is liable. For example, under the Transfer of Assets Rules, such continuing obligations include: (i) the transferee entity being required to remain as the beneficial owner of the assets transferred for at least two years (subject to certain limited exceptions); and (ii) the transferor and transferee entities being required to maintain their 'association' (as defined in the Transfer of Assets Rules) for at least two years.

7.3 Goods and Services Tax

[175] The goods and services tax (GST) was first introduced in Singapore on 1 April 1994 as an ad valorem tax. Currently, GST is levied at the rate of 7%. In the Singapore Budget Statement 2022, it was announced that the GST rate will be increased from 7% to 8% with effect from 1 January 2023, and from 8% to 9% with effect from 1 January 2024.

[176] Generally, GST is chargeable on taxable supplies made by taxable persons in the course of furtherance of any business carried on by that person. Disposal of business assets or liabilities (whether or not in connection with its reorganization) is deemed a supply made in the course or furtherance of that business under the Goods and Services Tax Act 1993 (the GSTA). Broadly speaking, a taxable person is a person who is liable to register or is registered under the GSTA. This, in turn, generally refers to a person who makes or expects to make taxable supplies exceeding SGD1 m over four successive quarters.

[177] A taxable supply is generally a supply of goods or services in Singapore other than an exempt supply under the GSTA. The sale of residential property, for example, is an exempt supply and is therefore not subject to GST. The transfer of ownership of shares in a company is also an exempt supply.

[178] Accordingly, if a transaction involves the disposal of business assets by a taxable person, there may be GST payable when the acquirer acquires the assets, which the acquirer may be able to recover as input tax provided that it is GST-registered and that certain stipulated conditions are met (e.g., the input tax is incurred for the making of taxable supplies, subject to certain exceptions), and there may again be GST payable if the acquirer is to sell the assets subsequently.

[179] However, the transfer of a business as a whole or part thereof as a going concern is treated as an excluded transaction, that is to say, it is neither a supply of goods nor services. As a result, such a transfer is not subject to GST. A transfer may be treated as a transfer of a business as a going concern and, therefore, an excluded transaction where the following conditions are satisfied:

- the supply of assets is made in connection to the transfer of a business or part thereof to the transferee;
- the transferred assets must be intended for use by the transferee to carry on the same business of the transferor;
- if only a part of the business is transferred, this portion must be capable of independent operation;
- after the transfer is completed, there must be continuity of the business. There must be no cessation of the business unless the cessation is temporary as may be necessary to allow the business to be operationally ready under the new ownership;
- the transferee must be a GST-registered person at the time of the transfer, or immediately becomes a taxable person as a result of the transfer (in the latter instance, the GST registration of the transferee shall be backdated to the date of the transfer); and
- both the transferor and transferee must keep proper records of the values and descriptions of the assets or class of assets transferred so as to allow both the transferor and transferee to reconcile the difference in the values of the assets before and immediately after the transfer with the value of the transferred assets.

[180] In the event that GST is payable, the parties can contractually decide who is to bear the GST, but the vendor is responsible for accounting for the GST to be charged to the IRAS.

[181] GST on imported services was introduced on 1 January 2020 to ensure a level playing ground by generally giving the same GST treatment to imported and local services. For imported services provided by a business outside Singapore to a GST-registered business in Singapore, GST is charged through a reverse charge mechanism if the GST-registered business in Singapore is not entitled to full input tax credits. In such circumstances, the Singapore entity is to account to the Singapore tax authority for GST chargeable on such services provided to it. In addition, for imported digital services between a business outside Singapore and a customer in Singapore, foreign businesses with a global turnover exceeding SGD1 m per annum and making supplies of digital services to customers in Singapore exceeding SGD100 000 per annum, including electronic marketplace operators, will be required to register for GST and such services will be subject to GST through an overseas vendor registration (OVR) regime. With effect from 1 January 2023, GST will be extended to: (a) the import of low value goods, i.e., up to SGD400 imported via air or post, which were previously not subject to GST; and (b) business-to-customer (B2C) imported non-digital services. For GST imposed on the import of goods, GST will be imposed through the current OVR and reverse charge regimes. For B2C imported non-digital services, GST will be imposed through the OVR regime.

7.4 Withholding Taxes

[182] With effect from 1 January 2008, all Singapore-resident companies are under the one-tier corporate tax system (the 'One-Tier System'). Under the One-Tier System, the tax on corporate profits is final, and dividends paid by a Singapore-resident company are tax-exempt in the hands of a shareholder (regardless of whether the recipients of such dividends are individuals or corporate entities) and no Singapore withholding tax will be imposed on such dividends, even though withholding tax rates on dividends are provided under some of the tax treaties to which Singapore is a party. The IRAS has clarified that the use of foreign-sourced income by Singapore-resident companies for the purpose of paying one-tier dividends to their shareholders outside Singapore (without such amounts being brought into Singapore) should not result in such foreign-sourced income being deemed to be remitted, and accordingly taxable in Singapore.

[183] Aside from dividends, the Income Tax Act provides for withholding of tax in respect of certain payments made to persons not known to be resident in Singapore. The withholding tax rate for such payments made to non-residents (excluding individuals) is normally either:

- the specified rate as stipulated in the Income Tax Act, which ranges from 10% to 22% of the gross amount depending on the nature of the payment (and whether the payment is derived by the recipient otherwise than from a trade, business, profession or vocation carried on or exercised by such person in Singapore and is not effectively connected with any permanent establishment in Singapore of that person); or
- the reduced tax rate as provided under a tax treaty (where applicable).

[184] The payments subject to withholding of tax under the Income Tax Act include:

- interest, commission, and fees in connection with any loan or indebtedness;
- royalty or other payments for the use of or the right to use any movable property;
- payment for the use of or the right to use scientific, technical, industrial or commercial knowledge or information or for the rendering of assistance or service in connection with the application or use of such knowledge or information;
- any payment for the management or assistance in the management of any trade, business or profession;
- rent or other payments for the use of any movable property;
- payment of remuneration to a non-resident director;
- consideration paid for real property to a non-resident seller who is a property trader; and

– certain professional service fees.

[185] Where the acquisition of a target company is financed through the issuance or acquisition of debt, any payments in the nature of interest which are borne by a person or permanent establishment in Singapore and paid to a person not known to be resident in Singapore could potentially be subject to withholding tax in Singapore. However, the applicable withholding tax rates may be reduced by tax treaties, and certain exemptions from withholding tax are available where the interest is paid to certain qualifying entities (e.g., branches in Singapore of foreign companies).

[186] Depending on the circumstances, there may be applicable exemptions or exclusions from the withholding tax obligation as discussed above. For example, where the acquisition of a target company is financed through the issuance of debt securities, the Qualifying Debt Securities (QDS) Scheme may be applicable, whereby issuers may make payments of interest and other qualifying income free of withholding tax, subject to conditions being met. Further, certain concessionary rates of tax and tax exemptions are available for holders of debt securities which are 'QDS' in nature.

8 TAX INCENTIVES FOR FOREIGN INVESTMENT

[187] Notwithstanding the prevailing corporate tax rate of 17% mentioned above, a number of tax incentive schemes and grants are available in Singapore. Such incentives are important in the context of mergers and acquisitions for a number of reasons. First, a Singapore target company may have been accorded certain tax incentives, and it may be necessary to ensure that such incentives would continue to apply post-merger or acquisition. Second, an acquiring entity may itself consider applying for or utilizing the available tax incentives in Singapore in order to enjoy a more favourable tax rate than the aforementioned 17% corporate tax rate.

[188] The tax incentive schemes available in Singapore tend to be targeted at specific industries or activities. They are administered by various governmental bodies in Singapore, including the Maritime and Port Authority of Singapore (MPA), Enterprise Singapore, the Singapore Economic Development Board (EDB), as well as the MAS and the IRAS. It should be noted that incentives are generally awarded at the discretion of the granting authority and are typically subject to ongoing review by such authorities over the life of the grant or award. Where share or business sales are concerned, it should be noted that where the target or transferor entity has been awarded a tax incentive, it may not necessarily follow that such incentive would continue to apply post-transfer. Generally, in a share sale, any tax incentives which the target enjoys may continue to be applicable after the sale, unless the incentive concerned is premised on, *inter alia*, who the shareholder(s) of the target is(are) or is subject to a 'no change of control' condition. Typically, in a business sale, any tax incentives awarded to the transferor would not automatically be transferred to the purchaser, and the purchaser would need to reapply for the incentives afresh. Thus, where any such tax incentives have been accorded to either a target entity or the transferor of a business, it would be important to consult with and update the relevant granting authority on any intended merger or acquisition.

[189] Various tax incentives available in Singapore are set out below.

8.1 Manufacturing and Services

[190] *Pioneer Incentive Scheme:* This incentive is generally intended to encourage companies to grow capabilities and conduct new or expanded activities in Singapore. The Pioneer Incentive Scheme, which covers Pioneer Industries and Pioneer Service Companies (as defined in the Economic Expansion Incentives (Relief from Income Tax) Act 1967 (EEIA)), may provide a full corporate tax exemption on qualifying profits of approved companies for up to fifteen years and is administered by the EDB under the EEIA. In particular, the EEIA sets out certain specific qualifying activities which would be eligible for the grant of the Pioneer Service Company status (e.g., engineering or technical services, computer-based information and other computer-related services and the development or production of industrial designs). However, the authorities have the discretion under the EEIA to grant pioneer incentives in respect of other services, activities and industries as may be prescribed or approved, if such authorities consider that it would be expedient in the public interest to do so. The Pioneer Incentive Scheme generally does not apply to IP income (as defined in the EEIA).

[191] *Development & Expansion Incentive* (DEI): Under the DEI, a qualifying company may be taxed at a reduced rate of either 5% or 10% on any 'expansion income' derived from certain qualifying activities. Typically, the initial tax relief period for the DEI is a maximum period of ten years and may be extended for up to five years at a time, to a maximum total period of twenty years. Tax relief under the DEI is granted on the additional (or 'expansion') income of the company which has been awarded the incentive. Briefly, the 'expansion income' of a qualifying company is the excess of the company's income from qualifying activities over its 'average corresponding income'. The 'average corresponding income' is, in turn, determined by taking the average of the company's total income derived from qualifying activities for the three years immediately preceding the commencement day of the incentive (or, where applicable, the three years immediately preceding the date of an extension or further extension of the tax relief period under the DEI). The incentive is administered by the EDB under the EEIA. The DEI generally does not apply to IP income (as defined in the EEIA).

[192] *Investment Allowance:* Qualifying expenditure under the Investment Allowance scheme may include fixed capital expenditure to be incurred on factory buildings in Singapore (excluding land); and the acquisition of know-how, patent rights, or productive equipment, among others. The scheme provides an allowance (in addition to any capital allowances) based on a percentage of approved fixed capital expenditure to be incurred for an approved project during a qualifying period of up to five to ten years (depending on the nature of the expenditure). Such allowance may be used by the qualifying company or corporate partnership to exempt equivalent amounts of income which are subject to tax.

8.2 Headquarter Activities

[193] *Headquarters Award*: Companies that carry out global or regional headquarters activities of managing, coordinating and controlling business activities for a group of companies may apply to the EDB for either the Pioneer Incentive Scheme or DEI described above. Such companies may be eligible for corporate tax exemption, or a concessionary tax rate of 5% or 10% on income derived from qualifying activities for an incentive period of five years, which may be extended subject to the company's commitment to undertake future expansion plans. Application for the award is open to companies that are prepared to make significant investments in contribution to the economy or in the advancement of capabilities towards globally leading industries. To qualify, companies must meet quantitative and qualitative criteria which include the employment created (including skills, expertise and seniority), total business expenditure, as well as a commitment to growing their capabilities (e.g., technology, skillsets, know-how) in Singapore.

8.3 Financial Services

[194] *Finance & Treasury Centre* (FTC): The FTC Incentive is aimed at encouraging corporations to use Singapore as a base for conducting treasury management activities for related companies in the region. Under this incentive, a concessionary tax rate of 8% (for awards granted after 24 March 2016) is available on fee income derived by the recipient company from its approved network companies for the provision of certain qualifying services and activities; as well as on certain interest income, dividends and gains from transactions in stocks and bonds, foreign exchange trading, interest rate swaps, financial futures and options. The incentive also provides a withholding tax exemption on interest payments on certain qualifying loans from, *inter alia,* banks and approved network companies. The concessionary tax treatment is available for a period of five years, and the award of the incentive may be extended subject to the recipient company's commitment to undertake further expansion plans in relation to its FTC activities/services. Applicant companies will be assessed on the quantitative and qualitative aspects of their proposed FTC operations. These include the employment created (including skills, expertise and seniority in the FTC team), total business expenditure which generates spin-offs to the economy, as well as the scale of the FTC operations in the depth and breadth of the services and activities. The FTC Incentive is administered by the EDB.

[195] *Financial Sector Incentive* (FSI): The FSI Scheme is a broad scheme intended to generally encourage and promote the development of the financial services sector in Singapore. The FSI Scheme provides concessionary corporate tax rates (of 5%, 10%, 12% or 13.5% (for awards granted after 1 June 2017), depending on the award granted) on income derived from qualifying financial services conducted in Singapore. Awards may be available under the FSI Scheme for fund management companies, headquarter services companies, capital market companies, credit syndication companies, and trustee companies, among others. Different requirements would have to be met by the approved companies depending on the type of award granted. For example, an approved fund management company would specifically be required to have a certain level of assets under management, but this requirement would not be applicable to other categories of approved FSI companies. The FSI Scheme is administered by the MAS.

[196] *Fund Incentive Schemes:* The location of fund management activities in Singapore could potentially create tax exposure in Singapore for the funds which are managed. In order to mitigate such risks, and in order to encourage and grow the fund management industry in Singapore, certain tax incentive schemes are available for both Singapore and non-Singapore tax resident funds which are managed by Singapore-based fund managers. Specified income of qualifying funds derived from a prescribed list of designated investments may be exempt from tax under the fund management incentive schemes. Various conditions are required to be met by both the fund and fund manager, and these may include commitments to make annual declarations to the authorities and investors of the fund. Generally, funds which have been awarded such incentives are not permitted to alter their investment strategies, unless approval has been sought from the relevant authorities. These incentive schemes are administered by the MAS and IRAS.

8.4 Trading Activities

[197] *Global Trader Programme* (GTP): The GTP incentive is available to companies based in Singapore which are engaged in international trading of qualifying products and commodities. The GTP incentive is generally intended for well-established international players, engaged in international physical trading on a principal basis who wish to establish their trading base in Singapore. The GTP incentive offers a concessionary tax rate of 5% or 10% on qualifying trading income, such as profits from qualifying transactions in specified commodities (e.g., petroleum and petroleum products; agricultural commodities and bulk edible products; and building and industrial materials). Generally, in order to qualify for the award of the GTP Incentive, an applicant must have substantial operations in Singapore and meet stringent quantitative criteria (including employment and local expenditure). Larger players with more established operations in Singapore should also perform strategic functions, such as compliance and risk management, financial, derivatives and logistics management. Companies must also be committed to making significant use of the banking, financial infrastructure, logistics, arbitration and other supporting services in Singapore, as well as contribute to manpower development in Singapore. The GTP incentive is administered by Enterprise Singapore.

8.5 Aircraft

[198] *Aircraft Leasing Scheme* (ALS): The ALS is generally intended for approved companies incorporated and resident in Singapore, or registered BTs which carry on the business of leasing aircraft or aircraft engines. The ALS provides a reduced corporate tax rate of 8% (for awards granted after 1 April 2017) on qualifying income derived from Singapore, from the leasing of aircraft or aircraft engines and other prescribed activities, for a period of up to five years. It also provides an automatic withholding tax exemption on qualifying payments on certain foreign loans for the purchase of aircraft or aircraft engines, subject to the fulfilment of certain conditions. The ALS and the automatic withholding tax exemption are administered by the EDB.

8.6 Insurance

[199] *Insurance and Reinsurance Companies*: Under the Insurance Business Development scheme, general, life and composite insurers and reinsurers may enjoy a concessionary tax rate of 10% for five years on qualifying income derived from qualifying insurance and reinsurance business activities conducted from Singapore.

8.7 Maritime

[200] Maritime Sector Incentive (MSI) (which includes: (i) the MSI-Approved International Shipping Enterprise (MSI-AIS) Award; (ii) the MSI-Maritime Leasing (MSI-ML) Award and; (iii) the MSI-Shipping-related Support Services (MSI-SSS) Award): Under the MSI Scheme, various awards are available to encourage, among others: (i) international ship owners and ship operators to establish their commercial shipping operations in Singapore; (ii) entities to use Singapore as their capital and funding base to finance their vessels or sea containers; and (iii) the growth of ancillary shipping service providers and to encourage shipping conglomerates to set up their corporate services functions in Singapore.

[201] Approved companies may enjoy tax concessions or tax exemptions on qualifying income for varying periods, depending on the type of award granted (e.g., approved international shipping enterprises that have been granted the MSI-AIS Award may enjoy tax exemptions on qualifying income, such as income from towing or salvage operations carried out from outside the limits of the port of Singapore by any foreign ship, for a renewable period of ten years). Withholding tax exemptions may also be available for interest payments for qualifying loans from foreign lenders for approved companies under most of the awards under the MSI Scheme, subject to conditions. These withholding tax exemptions have been extended to cover payments in respect of finance leases, hire-purchase arrangements, and loans used to finance equity injections into wholly owned Special Purpose Vehicles (SPVs) or intercompany loans to wholly owned SPVs for prescribed qualifying purposes. The MSI Scheme is administered by the MPA.

8.8 R&D Activities and IP-Related Incentives

[202] *Writing Down Allowances for IP Rights:* Entities which have incurred capital expenditure in acquiring certain IP rights, such as patents, copyright, and trademarks, for use in their trade or business are entitled to write down such expenditure fully over a period of either five, ten or fifteen years (as such entity may elect), subject to conditions being met.

[203] *IP Development Incentive* (IDI): Under the IDI, an approved company is eligible for a reduced corporate tax rate of either 5% or 10% on a prescribed percentage of qualifying IP income derived by the approved company during the incentive period. The concessionary tax rate will increase by 0.5% at prescribed regular intervals. Application for the IDI is open to companies that are prepared to make significant investments in contribution to the Singapore economy or in the advancement of capabilities towards globally leading industries. Applicants should have a good track record and are required to carry out expansionary projects in Singapore. In addition, applicants have to meet the prescribed economic commitment thresholds in relation to fixed asset investment or total annual business expenditure, and the number of skilled jobs created. The IDI is administered by the EDB.

8.9 General

[204] 'GST' *and Special Economic Zones:* Generally, all goods (except certain investment precious metals) which are imported into Singapore are subject to GST, regardless of whether the importer is GST-registered. Such import GST is collected by the Singapore Customs at the point of importation. However, import GST is suspended where the goods concerned are imported or housed in certain designated areas, such as in free trade zones, or in zero-GST and licensed warehouses, while under the control of Singapore Customs. The current GST rate is 7%, which will be increased to 8% with effect from 1 January 2023 and to 9% with effect from 1 January 2024.

With effect from 1 January 2020, GST is applicable to the importation of services in the context of business-to-business transactions by way of a reverse charge mechanism (the 'Reverse Charge Regime') where under certain prescribed circumstances GST-registered recipients of services from overseas suppliers may be required to account for GST on the value of such imported services as if they were the suppliers and non-GST registered persons who procure services from overseas suppliers would be liable for GST registration if certain prescribed conditions are met. With effect from 1 January 2023, the Reverse Charge Regime will be extended to cover the import of prescribed low value goods (generally goods imported by air or post with a value not exceeding SGD400).

[205] Also, with effect from 1 January 2020, GST is applicable to imported digital services in the context of business-to-consumer transactions by way of an OVR regime where persons who belong outside Singapore would be required to register for GST purposes where the prescribed conditions are met. With effect from 1 January 2023, the OVR Regime will be extended to all imported 'remote services' (whether digital or not) in the context of business-to-consumer transactions as well as the import of low value goods.

Relief from import GST is granted in respect of certain prescribed scenarios (such as low value goods, excluding intoxicating liquors and tobacco which are imported by air or post and have a total value not exceeding SGD400). However, please take note of our comments above on the application of the Reverse Charge Regime and OVR to the importation of low value goods.

Certain specific schemes are also available to qualifying importers, which allow for the suspension of the payment of GST at the point of importation. These schemes may be available generally (e.g., the Major Exporter Scheme), or may be industry-specific (e.g., the Approved Third Party Logistics Company Scheme and the Approved Refiner and Consolidator Scheme).

9 EMPLOYMENT CONSIDERATIONS

9.1 Employee Rights

[206] Employment law in Singapore is governed by statute, as well as the common law. The common law or case law in Singapore governing employment contracts and the employer-employee relationship is generally the same as in England. The common law position has been modified to some extent by statute in Singapore.

[207] The primary statute governing employment in Singapore is the Employment Act 1968 (the 'Employment Act'). The Employment Act generally applies to all employees, with the exception of seafarers, domestic workers, persons employed by a statutory board, and any class of persons that the Minister for Manpower declares, by notification in the *Gazette*, as not covered by the Employment Act. The Employment Act also applies to employees who are foreigners as long as they fall within the definition of 'employee' under the Employment Act.

[208] The Employment Act addresses several aspects of the employer-employee relationship and stipulates certain minimum terms and conditions of employment, such as statutory annual leave and sick leave, statutory protection against wrongful dismissal and the provision of key employment terms. Part IV of the Employment Act which governs, *inter alia,* rest days, hours of work and overtime pay, applies only to workmen whose basic salary is not more than SGD4 500 per month and employees (other than workmen and persons employed in managerial or executive positions) whose basic salary is not more than SGD2 600 per month (the 'Part IV Employees').

[209] Save for prescribed statutory obligations under the Employment Act and other employment-related legislation (as set out below), employer-employee relationships or aspects thereof are generally governed by the common law.

[210] Aside from the Employment Act, other Acts relevant to employment in Singapore include the Central Provident Fund Act 1953 (the CPF Act), Child Development Co-Savings Act 2001, Employment of Foreign Manpower Act 1990, Industrial Relations Act 1960 (IRA), Retirement and Re-Employment Act 1993, Trade Unions Act 1940, Trade Disputes Act 1941, Work Injury Compensation Act 2019, and Workplace Safety and Health Act 2006.

9.2 Compulsory Transfer of Employees

[211] When a merger or acquisition takes place, issues may arise as to the status of the employees within the new entity or the acquired company.

[212] Where the transaction involves the acquisition of shares in a company, the transaction will not affect the terms of the employment contract between the employees of the acquired company and the acquired company. The company in question continues as the same legal entity in spite of the change in shareholding or change in control. There is no automatic termination or variation of the terms of the employee's employment contract by operation of the law as a result of the transaction, and the employee would carry on as an employee of the same company after the completion of the share acquisition.

[213] Where the transaction involves an acquisition of a business as a going concern in Singapore, the business would be transferred by the transferor/employer company (the 'Transferor') to the acquirer/transferee company (the 'Transferee').

[214] In such a situation, to the extent that the Employment Act applies to the employees of the Transferor, section 18A(1) of the Employment Act has the effect of transferring the contract of service of such employees to the Transferee as if it was originally entered into with the Transferee. The period of employment of such employee with the Transferor at the time of the transfer will count as a period of employment with the Transferee, i.e., the transfer does not break the continuity of the period of employment.

[215] In addition:

(i) all of the Transferor's rights, powers, duties, and liabilities under or in connection with any such contract of service shall be transferred to the Transferee;

(ii) any act or omission performed prior to the transfer by the Transferor in respect of the contract of service is deemed to have been performed by the Transferee; and

(iii) any act or omission performed prior to the transfer by an employee employed in the undertaking or the part transferred in relation to the Transferor is likewise deemed to have been done in relation to the Transferee.

[216] The effect of the provisions of section 18A of the Employment Act is that there is an automatic statutory transfer of the employment of the employees together with the Transferor's business so that the Transferee is recognized in law as the new employer. The Transferee takes on all the rights and liabilities in respect of the employment contracts of the employees concerned.

[217] Section 18A(5) of the Employment Act requires the Transferor to notify its employees and the trade unions of such employees (if any) of the proposed transfer as soon as it is reasonable and before such a transfer takes place. This is to enable consultations between the Transferor and its employees and between the Transferor and the trade unions of such employees (if any) to take place.

[218] For completeness, we highlight that where the Employment Act does not apply to the employees, the transfer of such employees is a matter of contract between the Transferee and the employee, and is not automatic. The employment of such employees with the Transferor will also need to be terminated as a matter of contract between the Transferor and the employee (this can occur upon the completion of the acquisition by the Transferee).

9.3 Employee Reporting Obligations

[219] Employers in Singapore are generally required to include the details of the taxable remuneration and benefits derived by employees in the annual return of Employee's Remuneration (Form IR8A) unless arrangements have been made for such information to be transmitted directly to the IRAS. Singapore does not operate a 'pay-as-you-earn' system, and employees are responsible for directly paying the IRAS any applicable taxes in Singapore on the income earned from the exercise of employment in Singapore.

[220] Any foreign employee (who is: (i) neither a Singapore Citizen nor a Singapore Permanent Resident; or (ii) a Singapore Permanent Resident leaving Singapore permanently) who ceases employment, or who plans to leave Singapore for more than three months, is required to settle his tax liabilities before his departure from Singapore. Employers are required to report such impending cessation or departure to the IRAS as soon as it becomes known and will be required to withhold the payment of all monies due to the employee, pending tax clearance.

9.4 Termination of Employment

[221] At common law, a contract of service in relation to an employee may be terminated in one of the following ways.

[222] If a contract provides for employment for a fixed period of time, the contract will automatically come to an end when the term expires.

[223] A contract of service may be terminated by giving notice in accordance with the express terms of the contract (or in the absence of such express terms, in accordance with the Employment Act). It is common to provide for the period of notice required to terminate the employment contract and to provide for a right to payment in lieu of notice.

[224] A contract of service may be terminated summarily without notice by the employer. Summary dismissal of an employee without notice is a common law right of an employer, and the common reasons for such dismissal are misconduct, wilful disobedience or incompetence on the part of the employee.

[225] Note that where the Employment Act applies to the employee, such common law rights of termination are subject to the provisions of the Employment Act. In particular, the Employment Act stipulates the following:

(i) Either party to a contract of service may at any time give to the other party notice of his intention to terminate the contract of service (section 10(1)). This includes employees employed under fixed-term contracts.
(ii) Notice of intention to terminate a contract of service in relation to an employee must be in writing, whether given by the employer or the employee (section 10(5)).
(iii) The notice period may be mutually agreed between the employer and the employee in the contract of service, but the period of such notice must be the same for both parties (section 10(2)).
(iv) The following minimum notice periods apply if no notice period is set out in the contract (section 10(3)):
   (a) not less than one day's notice if the employee has been employed for less than twenty-six weeks;
   (b) not less than one week's notice if the employee has been employed for twenty-six weeks or more but less than two years;
   (c) not less than two weeks' notice if the employee has been employed for two years or more but less than five years; and
   (d) not less than four weeks' notice if the employee has been employed for five years or more.

[226] The Employment Act also provides that either party to a contract of service in relation to an employee may terminate the contract without notice or, if notice has been given, without waiting for the expiry of the notice period, by paying to the other party a sum equal to the salary at the gross rate of pay which would have accrued to the employee during the notice period (section 11(1)).

[227] Under the Employment Act, either party to a contract of service may also terminate the contract without notice in the event of a wilful breach of a condition of the contract by the other party (section 11(2)). In addition, the Employment Act provides that an employer may, after due inquiry, dismiss an employee without notice on the grounds of misconduct inconsistent with the fulfilment of the express or implied conditions of his service (section 14(1)). However, instead of dismissing the employee, the employer may elect to instantly downgrade the employee or instantly suspend him from work without payment of salary for a period not exceeding one week.

9.5 Retrenchment

[228] Retrenchment refers to the dismissal of an employee on the grounds of redundancy or by reason of any reorganization of the employer's profession, business, trade or work.

[229] There is generally no statutory requirement under Singapore law for an employer to pay retrenchment benefits to an employee. However, arrangements relating to retrenchment can be addressed in a contract of service and/or a collective agreement, and there are generally no restrictions on the terms of such arrangements.

[230] The Employment Act provides that a Part IV Employee who has been employed by his employer for less than two years is not entitled to any retrenchment benefits on the termination of his service on the ground of redundancy or by reason of any reorganization of the employer's profession, business, trade or work (section 45).

[231] There is a widespread misconception that section 45 of the Employment Act should, therefore, be construed as giving a Part IV Employee a right to retrenchment benefits if he has been employed for two years or more. However, it is quite clear that section 45 of the Employment Act is couched only in negative terms and does not create a statutory right to retrenchment benefits. Accordingly, where the contract of service is silent on retrenchment benefits and such provision is not made in a collective agreement, the Part IV Employee will not be entitled to right to retrenchment payments.

[232] While there is generally no statutory requirement to pay retrenchment benefits, employers in Singapore are expected to take into account the Tripartite Advisory on Managing Excess Manpower and Responsible Retrenchment (the 'Tripartite Advisory') issued by the Tripartite Alliance for Fair and Progressive Employment Practices. While the Tripartite Advisory does not have the force of law, it sets out employment practices which employers in Singapore are strongly encouraged to follow. It may be noted that the Tripartite Advisory recommends the payment of a retrenchment benefit varying between two weeks to one-month salary per year of service, depending on the financial position of the employer and taking into consideration the industry norm.

[233] Both retrenchment benefits and ex gratia payments given as compensation for loss of employment do not attract employer contributions to the CPF.

[234] Under the Employment (Retrenchment Reporting) Notification 2019 issued under the Employment Act, an employer who employs at least ten employees is required to notify the Ministry of Manpower if the employer has given any of its employees a notice of his or her retrenchment. Such notification must be given by the employer no later than five working days after the day that the employer gives such notice of retrenchment.

9.5.1 Labour Unions and Collective Labour Agreements

[235] The IRA, the Trade Unions Act 1940 and the Trade Disputes Act 1941 provide the legal framework for collective bargaining by trade unions on behalf of their members. The IRA sets out specific procedures for the negotiation of collective agreements (which embody agreements reached between trade unions and employers on matters pertaining to employees' terms and conditions of service), and the conciliation and arbitration of trade disputes arising from the collective bargaining process.

[236] Where an employee is represented by a trade union, which is recognized by the employer, the trade union or the employer may initiate the collective bargaining process by serving a notice in the prescribed form on the other party to negotiate a collective agreement in relation to any industrial matter (section 18 of the IRA). If the parties are not able to reach a collective agreement between themselves, the Commissioner for Labour will intervene to assist parties to reach an agreement by conciliation. If this is not possible, the matter will usually be referred to the Industrial Arbitration Court (IAC) which will settle the dispute by making rulings or awards that are final and binding.

[237] All collective agreements must be for an operative period of not less than two years and not more than three years (section 25(5) of the IRA). New agreements will thus have to be negotiated from period to period.

[238] After a collective agreement has been reached, it has to be certified by the IAC. An agreement so certified is deemed to be an award of the IAC which is binding on the employer (or its successor) and on the relevant trade union and its members (section 26 of the IRA).

[239] Some of the matters which are not negotiable under the process of collective bargaining are promotions, internal transfers (without prejudice to terms of employment), filling of appointment vacancies, termination of an employee's services by reason of redundancy or reorganization of the employer's profession, business, trade or work, the dismissal and reinstatement of an employee by an employer in circumstances in which the employee was dismissed without just cause and the assignment or allocation of duties or tasks to an employee consistent or compatible with the terms of his employment (section 18(2) of the IRA).

9.6 Social Security and Other Statutory Funds

9.6.1 Central Provident Fund

[240] The CPF is a comprehensive social security savings plan that is mandatory for all Singapore Citizens and Singapore Permanent Residents working in Singapore (the 'Local Employees'). Under the CPF Act, employers are required to make monthly contributions to the Local Employee's CPF account, calculated as a percentage of the Local Employee's salary. The CPF Act defines 'wages' as remuneration in money in respect of employment, and draws further distinctions between monthly wages and other forms of remuneration. The applicable rates of contribution vary depending on the amount of wages earned by the Local Employee and are subject to prescribed caps. The employer is then entitled, after making the requisite contributions to the CPF, to recover a prescribed amount from the monthly wages of the Local Employee.

[241] CPF contributions are not required, and in fact not allowed, in respect of the wages of foreign employees (i.e., employees that are not Local Employees). Employers who hire foreign employees will need to pay Foreign Worker Levy, but not CPF contributions. If a foreign employee is granted Singapore Permanent Resident status, he will be placed on the CPF scheme.

10 ACCOUNTING TREATMENT

10.1 Singapore Financial Reporting Standards Generally

[242] Singapore Financial Reporting Standards (the FRS) are prescribed by the Accounting Standards Council of Singapore. Generally, the FRS are adopted from the International FRS issued by the International Accounting Standards Board.

[243] Under the Companies Act, all companies incorporated under the Companies Act are generally required to prepare accounts or consolidated accounts in accordance with the FRS. However, the approval of the Registrar of Companies may be sought for any non-compliance with the FRS.

10.2 Acquisition Accounting

[244] FRS 103 *Business Combinations* applies for the accounting of any transaction in which an acquirer obtains control over one or more businesses. For the purpose of FRS 103, control is defined as the power to govern the financial and operating activities policies of an entity so as to obtain benefits from its activities. However, the concept of control is different under FRS 27 *Separate Financial Statements* and

FRS 110 *Consolidated Financial Statements*, i.e., an investor controls an investee when it is exposed, or has rights, to variable returns from its involvement with the investee and has the ability to affect those returns through its power over the investee.

[245] Where FRS 103 applies, the acquirer must apply the acquisition method of accounting. This means that goodwill may be recognized to the extent that the consideration paid for the acquisition exceeds the fair value of the assets acquired. FRS 103 does not apply to the formation of a joint venture, the acquisition of assets that do not constitute a business or a combination of entities or businesses already under common control – these transactions would not give rise to any goodwill.

[246] The acquisition method requires the acquirer to recognize the identifiable assets that are acquired, the liabilities assumed and any non-controlling interest (any minority interest in an acquired subsidiary). The identifiable assets and liabilities must be acquired as part of the business combination transaction and not from separate transactions. The identifiable assets recognized may be assets that are not recognized as assets by the acquiree, for example, intangible assets that were developed by the acquiree and not recognized as assets in the balance sheet of the acquiree.

[247] With certain exceptions (such as deferred tax assets or liabilities and liabilities for employee benefit arrangements), the identifiable assets and liabilities must be measured at their fair values on the date of acquisition. Non-controlling interests are measured either at fair value or at the non-controlling interest's proportionate share of the identifiable net assets.

[248] Goodwill is recognized by the acquirer to the extent that the consideration transferred for the acquisition, any non-controlling interest and any previously held equity interest in the acquiree (where the business combination is achieved in stages) exceeds the net value of the identifiable assets and liabilities acquired. Where the business combination is achieved in stages, all of the acquirer's previously held equity interest in the acquiree is revalued to fair value as at the date the acquirer obtains effective control over the acquiree (any revaluation gain or loss is recognized in profit or loss).

[249] In the case of a bargain purchase, the net value of the identifiable assets and liabilities acquired would exceed the consideration, any non-controlling interest and any previously held equity interest in the acquiree (where the business combination is achieved in stages). Such gain is recognized in profit or loss on the acquisition date.

[250] In this regard, consideration (including contingent consideration) is measured at fair value on the date of acquisition.

[251] If the initial accounting for a business combination cannot be completed by the end of the accounting period in which the business combination occurs, provisional amounts are reported in the financial statements for the accounting period. The provisional amounts will be retrospectively adjusted as new information is obtained by the acquirer over a measurement period (not exceeding one year from the acquisition date) on facts and circumstances that existed on the acquisition date.

[252] Transaction costs, including finder's fees, advisory, legal, accounting, valuation or other professional fees, are recognized as expenses in profit or loss.

10.3 Merger Accounting

[253] As mentioned, mergers involving entities under common control will fall outside the scope of FRS 103 because there is no change of control. The acquisition method of accounting would not be appropriate, and no goodwill should be recognized in such a merger.

[254] Where the entities are parent and subsidiary, the parent would generally be required to prepare consolidated accounts or financial statements under FRS 110 *Consolidated Financial Statements*. Consolidated financial statements refer to the financial statements of a group in which the assets, liabilities, equity, income, expenses and cash flows of the parent and its subsidiaries are presented as those of a single economic entity. Consolidated accounts are required of a parent under FRS 110 unless: (i) it itself is a subsidiary whose other owners have been informed about, and are agreeable to such parent not presenting consolidated financial statements; (ii) its debt or equity instruments are not publicly-traded; (iii) it did not make any regulatory filings of financial statements for the purpose of issuing any class of instruments in a public market and; (iv) its ultimate or intermediate parent produces publicly available consolidated financial statements. Investment entities are also not required to consolidate subsidiaries or apply FRS 103 when they obtain control of another entity, and would instead be required to measure investments in such subsidiaries at fair value through profit and loss in accordance with FRS 109 *Financial Instruments*.

[255] As far as measurement is concerned under FRS 110, an entity is required to include the income and expenses of a subsidiary in its consolidated financial statements, from the date it gains control until the date when such entity ceases to control the subsidiary.

11 EMERGING ISSUES AND FUTURE DEVELOPMENTS

[256] The Take-over Code was amended on 25 January 2019 to clarify its application to companies with a dual-class share structure ('DCS companies') that are primarily listed on the SGX-ST.

A typical company with a DCS structure would have shares which carry one vote in each class (OV shares) and shares which carry multiple votes each in another class (MV shares). MV shares of a DCS company listed on the SGX-ST may be held by an individual or a group of persons or an entity ('permitted holder group'). The holder of MV shares must be appointed as a director of the listed DCS company

('Responsible Director'), or in the case of a permitted holder group, a Responsible Director must be appointed for the group. The MV shares may be converted into OV shares, voluntarily by the holders of MV shares ('Voluntary Conversion') or automatically, on a one-for-one basis, if a Responsible Director ceases to be a director (or in the case of a permitted holder group, where a new Responsible Director is not appointed), or the MV share is sold or transferred to any person (or in the case of a permitted holder group, to a person who is not in the permitted holder group) ('Automatic Conversion') unless a waiver of such Automatic Conversion is approved by independent shareholders at a general meeting where one MV share is limited to only one vote. Holders of MV shares may seek to reduce the number of voting rights attached to each MV share ('Reduction').

Rule 14.1 of the Take-over Code provides that, except with SIC's consent, any person who:

- acquires shares which carry 30% or more of the voting rights of a company; or
- together with persons acting in concert with him, holds not less than 30% but not more than 50% of the voting rights, and such person, or any person acting in concert with him, acquires in any period of six months additional shares carrying more than 1% of the voting rights, is required to make a mandatory offer for the remaining voting rights in the company.

A Voluntary Conversion or an Automatic Conversion (each, a 'Conversion'), or a Reduction will lower the total number of voting rights of a DCS company, which may result in an increase in the percentage of voting rights of a shareholder of the DCS company and persons acting in concert with him.

The following are highlights of some of the changes to the Take-over Code in light of the foregoing:

(1) Duty to make mandatory offer triggered by the conversion of shares in one class which carry MV shares into shares in another class which carry only one vote each (OV shares): The Take-over Code provides that an increase in the percentage of voting rights of such a shareholder or group of shareholders acting in concert ('Triggering Shareholder') amounts to an acquisition for the purpose of Rule 14.1 of the Take-over Code. Therefore, the Triggering Shareholder is required to make a mandatory offer under the Take-over Code. The offer price will be the highest price that the Triggering Shareholder has paid for voting rights in the DCS company in the six months prior to the earlier of the date of the announcement of the Conversion or Reduction or the date of the Conversion or the Reduction ('relevant date'). If the Triggering Shareholder did not acquire shares in the DCS company in the six months prior to the relevant date, SIC would generally require the offer price to be the simple average of the daily volume-weighted average traded prices of the DCS company on the latest twenty trading days prior to the relevant date.

(2) Duty to make mandatory offer waived for shareholder independent of Conversion or Reduction: The obligation to make a mandatory offer

under Rule 14 of the Take-over Code is waived for a Triggering Shareholder who is independent of a Conversion or a Reduction. The Take-over Code provides that the independent Triggering Shareholder must not acquire additional voting rights in the DCS company after becoming aware that the Conversion or Reduction is imminent or exercise the voting rights in excess of the relevant mandatory offer thresholds under Rule 14 of the Take-over Code from the date of the Conversion or Reduction. In the SIC Response, SIC stated that whether or not a Triggering Shareholder is independent would depend on the specific circumstances of a Conversion or a Reduction. Therefore, the Triggering Shareholder should consult SIC in all relevant cases and explain why he should be regarded as independent. SIC has indicated that a Triggering Shareholder would not be deemed not independent of a Conversion or a Reduction solely because he voted in favour of the Conversion or Reduction.

(3) Duty to make a mandatory offer may be waived in certain circumstances for shareholders not independent of Conversion or Reduction: SIC will grant a waiver from the requirement for the Triggering Shareholder to make a mandatory offer under Rule 14, subject to the approval of the independent shareholders of the DCS company for a Whitewash Resolution being obtained either before or within three months after the date of the Conversion or the Reduction. The Whitewash Resolution is a separate resolution that is approved at a general meeting of the DCS company by a majority of the independent shareholders, on a poll, waiving their rights to receive a takeover offer. Alternatively, in lieu of making a mandatory offer under Rule 14, SIC will allow the Triggering Shareholder to dispose of such number of shares as is necessary to reduce his aggregate voting rights in the DCS company to below the thresholds stipulated in Rule 14.1 within six months of the date of the Conversion or the Reduction (or such longer time period as SIC may allow in exceptional circumstances).

(4) Offer price for MV shares and OV shares in the takeover offer should be the same: When making a takeover offer for a DCS company, an offeror may have to make an offer for both MV shares and OV shares. The Take-over Code provides that where a company has more than one class of equity share capital, a comparable offer must be made for each class of shares. In the case where traded prices are not available for all the classes of equity shares and those classes of shares differ only in their voting rights (which would be the case for MV shares and OV shares), the offer price for MV shares and OV shares should be the same. In all other cases, the relative offer prices would need to be justified to SIC in advance.

[257] Under the Listing Manual, an issuer listed on the SGX-ST ('ListCo') may seek a voluntary delisting from the SGX-ST, subject to the requisite majority of its shareholders approving the resolution to delist the ListCo ('Voluntary Delisting Resolution') and the ListCo offering a reasonable exit alternative to its shareholders and the holders of any other classes of listed securities to be delisted ('Exit Offer').

The Listing Manual was revised on 11 July 2019 to provide clarification on the application of the revised voluntary delisting and Exit Offer requirements to voluntary liquidation, the scheme of arrangement or a general offer under the Take-over Code:

(1) *Voluntary Delisting Resolution Requirements.* Under the revised SGX-ST Listing Rules, SGX-ST may agree to a voluntary delisting application by a ListCo if the Voluntary Delisting Resolution has been approved by a majority of at least 75% of the ListCo's total number of issued shares (excluding treasury shares and subsidiary holdings) held by the shareholders present and voting at the general meeting of the ListCo. To enhance minority shareholder protection, the offeror and parties acting in concert with it ('Offeror Concert Party Group') are required to abstain from voting on the Resolution.

The requirement that the Voluntary Delisting Resolution not be voted against by 10% or more of the ListCo's total number of issued shares (excluding treasury shares and subsidiary holdings) held by the shareholders present and voting at the general meeting of the ListCo has been removed. This is to strike a balance between ensuring that minority shareholders are not unduly prejudiced and the power accorded to the minority shareholders is not unduly disproportionate (since the Offeror Concert Party Group must now abstain from voting).

(2) *Exit Offer Requirements.* The Listing Manual has been enhanced such that an Exit Offer must not merely be reasonable; it must also be fair. The practice to require the Exit Offer to include a cash alternative as the default alternative has also been codified as a Listing Rule requirement.

The Listing Manual requires a ListCo to appoint an IFA to advise on the Exit Offer, and the IFA must opine that the Exit Offer is fair and reasonable. To ensure that IFA opinions are well understood by investors, SGX-ST expects that the bases for determining fairness, as well as the reasonableness of the Exit Offer, be detailed separately, where appropriate.

(3) *Application of Voluntary Delisting Resolution and Exit Offer Requirements to the Scheme of Arrangement.* The Voluntary Delisting Resolution requirements do not apply to a delisting pursuant to a scheme of arrangement under the Singapore Companies Act because the voting requirements under the Singapore Companies Act are comparable.

However, the Exit Offer requirements (including the requirement for cash alternative in an Exit Offer) apply to a delisting pursuant to a scheme of arrangement as such requirements are not found in the Singapore Companies Act. In practice, this is not an issue since most schemes of arrangement involve a cash consideration only. In those rare schemes which involve a securities consideration, the cash Exit Offer requirements may be waived if the securities are (or are to be) listed on the SGX-ST and constitute most of the consideration on offer.

(4) *Waiver of Voluntary Delisting Resolution and Exit Offer Requirements in a Phase 2 Delisting.* In a number of cases, an offeror makes a takeover offer ('Offer')

for a target with a view to reaching the 90% compulsory acquisition threshold. If the offeror falls short of that 90% threshold, the offeror may lapse the Offer or waive the condition and declare the Offer unconditional with the Offeror Concert Party Group holding anywhere between 50% + 1 and 90% – 1 of all the ListCo shares (assuming the Offeror Concert Party Group holds no ListCo shares prior to the Offer). In the latter case, the offeror sometimes proceeds to try to delist the ListCo ('Phase 2 Delisting'). In a Phase 2 Delisting, it is usual to seek a waiver of the requirement for the Voluntary Delisting Resolution.

Here, the SGX-ST has stated that the waiver would only be considered if the offeror has received 'acceptances' in respect of 75% or more of all the ListCo shares (excluding those held by the Offeror Concert Party Group). Previously, the waiver is generally granted if the Offeror Concert Party Group holds 90% or more of the ListCo shares as at the close of the Offer and it does not matter whether those shares were held prior to the Offer, were acquired from market purchases or were acceptances to the Offer. Thus, an Offeror Concert Party Group which holds more than 90% of all the ListCo shares as at the close of the Offer (but falls short of the 90% compulsory acquisition threshold) may now still not be able to obtain a waiver of the requirement for the Voluntary Delisting Resolution.

(5) *Application of Voluntary Delisting Resolution and Exit Offer Requirements to Other Privatization Mechanisms.* The Voluntary Delisting Resolution and Exit Offer requirements do not apply to a delisting pursuant to a:
   (a) voluntary liquidation; or
   (b) general offer made under the Take-over Code where the offeror is exercising its right of compulsory acquisition.

[258] Currently, Section 215(1) of the Companies Act provides that in the event that the Offeror acquires not less than 90% of the total number of shares of the target company (other than those already held by the Offeror, its related corporations or their respective nominees as at the date of the offer and excluding treasury shares), the Offeror will be entitled to exercise the right to compulsorily acquire all the shares of the target company from shareholders who have not accepted the offer at a price equal to the offer price.

The Companies Act Working Group has recommended that shares held or acquired by the following persons should be excluded from the computation of the 90% threshold for compulsory acquisition under section 215:

(a) a person who is accustomed or is under an obligation, whether formal or informal, to act in accordance with the directions, instructions or wishes of the Offeror in respect of the target company;
(b) a body corporate controlled by the Offeror;
(c) a person who is, or is a nominee of, a party to a share acquisition agreement with the Offeror;
(d) the Offeror's close relatives (i.e., spouse; children, including adopted children and step-children; parents; and siblings);

(e) a person whose directions, instructions or wishes the Offeror is accustomed or is under an obligation, whether formal or informal, to act in accordance with, in respect of the target company; and
(f) a body corporate controlled by a person described in (e).

www.ingramcontent.com/pod-product-compliance
Ingram Content Group UK Ltd.
Pitfield, Milton Keynes, MK11 3LW, UK
UKHW020151290926
15471UKWH00004B/813

9 789403 503066